Davina's
SUGAR-FREE
IN A HURRY

Davina's
SUGAR-FREE
IN A HURRY

Davina McCall

This book is dedicated to Sarah.
You are my person.

First published in Great Britain in 2016
by Orion Publishing Group Ltd
Carmelite House, 50 Victoria Embankment
London EC4Y 0DZ
An Hachette UK Company

10 9 8 7 6 5 4 3 2 1

A CIP catalogue record for this book is available from the British Library.

ISBN: 978 1 4091 5769 4

Food director and stylist: Anna Burges-Lumsden
Photographer: Andrew Hayes-Watkins
Props stylist: Sarah Birks
Project editor: Jinny Johnson
Proofreader: Elise See Tai
Indexer: Vicki Robinson
Food stylist's assistants: Lou Kenny, Charlotte O'Connell and Phil Wells
Thanks to www.linenme.com

Nutritional advice and analysis: Fiona Hunter, Bsc (Hons) Nutrition, Dip Dietetics

Printed and bound in Germany

Note: While every effort has been made to ensure that the information in this book is correct, it should not be substituted for medical advice. The recipes in this book should be used in combination with a healthy lifestyle. If you are concerned about any aspect of your health, speak to your GP. People under medical supervision should not come off their medication without speaking to their health professional.

The Orion Publishing Group's policy is to use papers that are natural, renewable and recyclable products and made from wood grown in sustainable forests. The logging and manufacturing processes are expected to conform to the environmental regulations of the country of origin.

www.orionbooks.co.uk

For more delicious recipes, features, videos and exclusives from Orion's cookery writers, and to sign up for our 'Recipe of the Week' email visit **bybookorbycook.co.uk**

Contents

Great food . . . in a hurry 7

1 **Light Meals and Soups** 16

2 **Speedy Salads** 44

3 **Easy Suppers** 64

4 **Weekend Specials** 98

5 **Guilt-free Snacks** 130

6 **Sweet Things** 164

Nutritional Information 204
My 5-Week Plan 212
Index 218

Great food . . . in a hurry

Life really is busy, isn't it?! We are all speeding around, trying our best to cook and eat healthily and feed our bodies what they need. But it's all too easy to let things slip when time is short and you need a good meal on the table quickly.

I am in a hurry. Most of the time.

So that's why I'm really excited about this new collection of refined sugar-free recipes – which are *completely* yummy. I've loved working with my team to develop these simple recipes that taste great and keep me and my family healthy and happy. The good news is that the ingredients don't cost the earth and the dishes don't take long to prepare and cook.

There's everything here from soups and salads and scrumptious suppers to the most delicious cakes and puddings for the occasional treat. I guarantee that my latest chocolate brownies are the moistest, squishiest ever.

So, let's get it on and cook something up . . . in a hurry.

I've learned so much since my first cookbook, *5 Weeks to Sugar-Free*. I'm loving cooking more and more – and I'm passionate about providing good healthy food for my family.

But OMG there's a bewildering amount of advice out there now. It seems like not only dietitians and chefs but also a whole gang of bloggers and home cooks are on Instagram and Twitter, telling us what and what not to eat, giving us their version of the latest superfood diet and what to do about yo-yoing blood sugar.

Good food doesn't have to involve crazy hard-to-find, expensive ingredients and huge amounts of time in the kitchen boiling up mysterious concoctions. Much as I love food and my family, I just don't have hours to spend on cooking.

I want fast, I want tasty, I want healthy.

Most of the recipes in this book don't involve chopping and stirring for hours and they use ingredients that you can find in most supermarkets. Yes, in the Weekend Specials chapter there are some recipes that take a bit longer, but that's mostly allowing time for meat to marinate to melting tenderness or for a stew to bubble its way to deliciousness in the oven. That means once you've done some speedy prep you can go off for a walk, a bike ride with the kids or even grab some me time, knowing that you'll come back to a fab meal.

What's important . . .

I'm not a scientist or a food expert, but I've found out so much from working on these books with great cooks and nutritionists. I'm convinced that preparing your own meals from food that is as fresh and unprocessed as possible is what really counts. That way you know exactly what you're eating and you can control your portions and your salt and sugar intake.

Try to avoid convenience foods such as ready meals, prepared sauces and shop-bought cakes and biscuits. Buy stuff that's had as little done to it as possible and you'll save money too. But that doesn't mean you can't use foods such as frozen peas and cans of beans and tomatoes, even ready-cooked quinoa and rice. They deserve a place in everyone's larder and they're great for getting a super-quick meal on the table – you'll see them crop up quite often in the recipes in this book for speed's sake.

Just get into the habit of checking the ingredients of anything you buy in a packet or tin. For example, look for cans of beans without added salt and sugar.

Nourishing food is a way of investing in yourself and your family. You're storing up good health for the future. Health problems might start later in life, but the damage can be done much earlier, and it's never too soon to start healthy eating. If you lay down the right habits for your children while they're young, they're more likely to eat well as they grow up.

Great reasons to eat well and cut down on refined and processed foods

- Helps you look younger and feel better – it just does!
- Helps build a strong body and maintain health.
- Helps you deal with stress and prevents energy dips.
- Helps you sleep properly and perform well the next day. If you don't sleep well you're more likely to crave junk food and get overweight.

Blood sugar, clean eating and superfoods – the lowdown

So everyone is talking about blood sugar now – and the rise in diabetes. I didn't really understand it all completely so I've talked to people who do. I've been back to Fiona, my lovely nutritionist, to get the lowdown on that and other things I'm not clear about.

D: Can you explain the whole blood sugar thing to me?

F: We all need some sugar – or glucose to be technically correct – in our blood because it supplies energy to the cells around the body, but the amount of glucose needs to be tightly controlled. Too much is bad news, but so is too little and the body has sophisticated mechanisms to control the levels.

During the digestive process, carbohydrates (like bread, rice and fruit) need to be broken down into glucose before they can be absorbed into the blood. After eating carbs, levels of glucose in the blood start to rise and once this happens the body responds by producing the hormone insulin, which takes glucose out of the blood into the cells, where it can be used for energy. Glucose levels in the blood then start to fall again. Any glucose that isn't used for energy by the cells is converted into something called glycogen and is stored – some in the muscles and some in the liver – but the rest is converted to fat, which is stored around the body.

When blood glucose drops below a certain level the body responds by producing another hormone called glucagon, which triggers the conversion of glycogen stored in the muscles into glucose. This is then released back into the bloodstream restoring levels to normal – that's how blood glucose levels are maintained at a normal range between meals.

D: So when I feel a bit weak and wobbly is that my blood sugar? And what do I do when I feel like that? It's tempting to reach for a chocolate bar, but I know that's bad!

F: When blood glucose levels start to drop, which is a condition called hypoglycaemia, you start to feel weak, wobbly and hungry. Other symptoms include poor concentration, dizziness and headaches and this is your body's way of telling you that you need to eat. There are couple of things you can do to reduce the risk of hypoglycaemia. The first is to eat little and often – have three small meals with a couple of healthy snacks in between. The second is to make sure you choose what nutritionists call 'slow release' or low GI carbs (smart carbs). These are carbohydrates that are digested and converted into glucose slowly so they produce a slow, steady supply of glucose into the bloodstream over a longer period of time. This way your blood has just enough glucose to keep it happy – not too much, not too little.

The Glycaemic Index is a term used to describe how quickly a carbohydrate is digested and converted into glucose in the blood. High GI carbs, like French bread, chips and mashed potato, are broken down into glucose very quickly so they cause a rapid spike in blood sugar levels, causing the body to respond by producing a big slug of insulin.

Low GI carbs, such as lentils or porridge oats, are digested and converted into sugar more slowly so they produce a gentle rise in blood sugar. This means that the body doesn't need to produce so much insulin to restore levels to normal.

D: So is the fact that so many people have a high GI diet why diabetes is getting to be so common?

F: Diabetes is certainly increasing and at an alarming level. About four million people in the UK now have diabetes (figures from Diabetes UK).

There are two types of diabetes – type 1 and type 2. Type 1 is more common in younger people and occurs when the pancreas stops producing insulin. The reason why this happens is not fully understood, but people with type 1 diabetes require regular insulin injections.

But 90 per cent of people with diabetes have type 2 diabetes, which is becoming more and more common, and experts believe this is probably due to lifestyle factors – obesity, lack of exercise and a poor diet. Unlike people with type 1 diabetes, people with type 2 produce some insulin, but either they are unable to produce enough or the body doesn't respond to the insulin produced in the way it should – a condition called insulin resistance. One theory is that if you eat a high GI diet your pancreas is constantly having to produce insulin to bring blood glucose back to normal levels and after a period of time it simply becomes worn out.

When the body can't produce enough insulin or it becomes resistant to insulin, glucose can't get into the cells and the level of glucose in the blood starts to rise. This can cause damage to blood vessels, nerves, eyes and kidneys and increase the risk of heart disease and stroke. The exact cause of insulin resistance is unknown but obesity – particularly excess fat around the waist – and inactivity are thought to be the primary causes.

Several studies have shown that lack of exercise increases the risk of insulin resistance and type 2 diabetes, but the good news is that physical activity/exercise helps to improve the body's ability to use/respond to insulin.

The muscles use more glucose than any other tissues in the body. When muscles are active they burn their stored glucose for energy and refill their stores with glucose taken from the blood, which helps to keep blood glucose levels in balance. Exercise also helps the muscles absorb glucose without the need for insulin so the more muscle your body has, the more glucose it can burn to control blood glucose levels

D: What's the best way of eating to keep my blood sugar under control?

F: Eat little and often, choose smart carbs and cut out refined foods such as white sugar, white flour and so on. Watch your portion size, keep your weight within the ideal range and keep active.

D: I keep hearing about 'clean eating' – what does it mean?

F: Clean eating means eating foods that are as close to the way that nature delivers them as possible. It doesn't mean cutting out wheat, gluten, or dairy; eating only raw or alkaline foods or food combining or balancing 'macros'. Eating 'clean' simply means basing your diet around wholefoods that are unprocessed or minimally processed, in season and as much as possible locally grown and organic. Heavily processed foods are usually foods that have been stripped of their nutrients, stuffed full of additives and extra salt, sugar or fats. You don't need a degree in nutrition to know that these foods can't be good for you and aren't the best way of fuelling your body.

D: What are superfoods?

F: To be honest, the term superfood has become a bit of a marketing gimmick. Although there's no legal or scientific definition of a superfood, most nutrition experts would define a superfood as any food that delivers an impressive amount of particular vitamins, minerals, antioxidants, phytochemicals, dietary fibre or healthy fats. They are foods that are known to help protect against a whole host of diseases, including cancer and heart disease as well as dementia and other diseases associated with ageing.

Superfoods don't have to be expensive or exotic – a carrot is a superfood. In fact most fruit and vegetables could be called superfoods. You'll find plenty of superfoods in the recipes in this book.

Sugar!

Sugar is the big concern. The latest guidelines from the World Health Organisation say that our intake of free sugars (that means added sugars, not the natural sugar in foods such as fruit and milk) should be under ten per cent of our total calorie intake. Ideally it should be below five per cent – or about six teaspoons a day. And don't forget that includes the sugar in foods such as chutneys, jams and sauces.

Avoid refined white sugar and when you do bake a sweet treat, use honey or dried fruit instead. Sweeten cakes with naturally sweet vegetables such as carrots and beetroot. This might sound odd at first, but they taste amazing – try the courgette cake or the carrot, apple and walnut cupcakes in the Sweet Things chapter. You'll find that the less sugar you have the less you will crave.

Tips to help you avoid refined sugar

- Check labels – watch out for foods that say they are 'sugar free' but contain artificial sweeteners. And look out for 'low-fat' foods, such as fruity yoghurts, that often contain lots of sugar.

- Stop eating savoury foods that contain sugar – such as ready-made sauces, canned soups and ketchup.

- Check the sugar content of some of the 'healthy' snacks such as energy bars. You'll be surprised at how much many contain. Make your own snacks instead, using recipes in this book.

- When you feel like something sweet, try having a drink of water or a herbal tea first. Often when you think you're hungry and want a snack you are actually just dehydrated. Once you've quenched your thirst the sweet craving may go away.

- If you still feel like something sweet, try having a small handful of nuts instead. They should sustain you and take away your desire for a sugar fix.

Hurry up – make a plan

Planning is key. I can cope with shopping and I enjoy cooking but sometimes it's the thinking what to have day after day that's the hardest bit. And it's easy to get stuck in a rut and just cook the same things over and over rather than trying something new. But if you think ahead and plan your week's meals in advance not only do you reduce stress but it also helps you balance your diet.

Get the whole family involved and ask them what they would like to eat. Get them to look through this book and pick out the dishes they fancy! There are plenty of yummy soups and salads, tasty snacks – even my favourite nachos! – and filling main meals such as fish crumble, lamb kebabs and slow-cooked pork. We also have a fab collection of puddings and cakes that are sweetened with honey, fruit and even veg such as carrot and sweet potato. You're going to love them. Eating well has never tasted so good. The recipes are quick to prepare. Some need a bit of time in the oven, but that's fine as you can be getting on with something else while they're cooking.

Healthy eating is more than just adding a banana to your breakfast or having a bit of lettuce with your supper. We all need to think more carefully about what we eat to make sure we have a good balanced diet, with plenty of fresh vegetables, good protein and healthy fats. I find that a good way of tackling this is to keep a food diary for a couple of weeks and write down everything I eat – and I mean everything! I've been known to forget that bag of crisps I scoffed while waiting for a train or that chocolate bar I stole from the kids' stash. If you really do write it all down, you can work out what your weak spots were, when you were tempted to eat junk and how you can improve your diet.

My 5-week plan

Cooking from the recipes in this book will help to keep you on the straight and narrow – avoiding sugar and refined carbs and eating plenty of smart carbs, veggies and good protein. If you want to calorie count, we've included calorie info on each page and there are full nutritional details at the end of the book, giving the carbohydrate, fat, protein, sugar and salt content of each recipe.

And if you want to lose weight, have a look at my 5-week plan at the back of the book for menus that will gradually reduce your calorie count and your sugar intake. We've made it easy for you!

What works for me . . .

- Avoid faddy diets – who's got the time? Eat a wide range of good fresh foods with plenty of vegetables and whole grains and you won't go far wrong.

- Eat whole dairy products. Go for whole milk and yoghurt, butter and cheese but in small amounts.

- Protein – include meat, fish, poultry, eggs and plant protein such as nuts and beans in your diet. Prepare them in healthy ways.

- Eat unrefined carbs. Carbohydrates are essential fuel for our brain, our nervous system and our organs. We need carbs in order to function so avoiding them altogether is not a sensible way of losing weight. Go for fibre-rich smart carbs such as beans, pulses, wholegrain bread and brown rice instead of white bread, white rice and pasta. Choose sweet potatoes rather than white.

- Avoid refined sugar. Sweeten cakes and puddings with honey or with naturally sweet fruit and vegetables.

- Watch your portions and don't overeat. If you feel like eating more once you've finished your meal, wait a while and give your body a chance to digest your food. You'll probably find you're perfectly satisfied.

A few cooking notes

- Peel garlic, onions and other vegetables unless otherwise specified. The weights given in the ingredients lists are the peeled weight.

- Stock is easy to make and there's a recipe in my *5 Weeks to Sugar-Free* book, but for speed's sake use the good ready-made fresh stocks you can buy in supermarkets now. Heat the stock first before adding it to your other ingredients – saves lots of time.

- I like to use free-range chicken and eggs whenever I can, but that's your call.

—1—

Light Meals and Soups

Red pepper toasties 19
Cheesy pea fritters with roasted cherry tomatoes 20
Asparagus and dippy eggs 23
Baked eggs Florentine 24
Home-made pot noodles 27
Nutty greens 28
Bean and chorizo soup 31
Roasted tomato and red pepper soup
with goat cheese toasts 32
Minty pea soup 35
Sunshine soup 36
Supergreen soup 39
Beetroot and apple soup 40
Cold tomato soup à la AJ 43

Red pepper toasties

Anything on toast goes down well with my family and this combo of ricotta and peppers seriously works. If you're really short of time, you can buy a jar of ready-roasted peppers and just drain them and cut them into strips.

1 Preheat your grill to high. Place the peppers cut-side down on a baking tray and put them under the grill for 8 minutes or until lightly charred. Tip the peppers into a bowl, cover the bowl with cling film and set it aside for 5 minutes. Then remove the skin from the peppers and cut them into strips.

2 Heat a griddle pan. Brush the slices of bread with a little olive oil and then griddle them on both sides on the hot pan. Rub the cut garlic clove over the griddled bread.

3 Spread each piece of bread with ricotta, scatter over some capers and then top with pepper strips. Add a few thyme leaves and a drizzle of balsamic vinegar, then season and serve while still hot.

Serves 4
234 calories per serving

2 red or 1 red and 1 yellow pepper, halved and deseeded
4 thick slices of sourdough bread
2 tbsp olive oil
1 garlic clove, cut in half
100g ricotta
2 tbsp capers, drained and rinsed
fresh thyme leaves
1 tbsp good-quality balsamic vinegar
salt and black pepper

Time check

Prep: 10 minutes
Cooking: 10 minutes

Cheesy pea fritters with roasted cherry tomatoes

Everyone loves fritters and these make a great quick supper for the kids – and me! If you like, you can make the fritters ahead of time and then warm them through in the oven before serving.

1 Preheat the oven to 200°C/Fan 180°C/Gas 6. Put the tomatoes in a shallow roasting tin and drizzle them with a little of the oil. Season the tomatoes with salt and pepper and roast them for 10 minutes.

2 Meanwhile, make the fritters. Crack the eggs into a large bowl, add all the other ingredients and mix them together thoroughly. Add a little more milk if the mixture seems too thick.

3 Heat a little oil in a large frying pan over a medium heat, then add tablespoons of the mixture to make fritters – 3 or 4 at a time. Fry them for 2 minutes, then flip them over and fry for another 2 minutes on the other side. Remove the cooked fritters with a slotted spatula, put them on a baking tray and keep them warm while you make the rest.

4 Serve topped with roasted tomatoes.

Davina's tip

These freeze well. Cook the fritters and leave them to cool completely, then pack them into a freezer-proof container with sheets of baking paper in between. Freeze for up to a month. Defrost the fritters and warm them through in the oven before serving.

Makes 12

143 calories per fritter

400g cherry tomatoes on the vine, cut into 4 branches
3 tbsp olive oil
2 large eggs, beaten
150g wholemeal spelt flour, sifted
1 tsp baking powder, sifted
200g cottage cheese
2 tbsp finely grated Parmesan cheese
pinch of cayenne pepper
200g frozen peas, defrosted
4 spring onions, sliced
75ml whole milk, plus extra if needed
salt and black pepper

Time check

Prep: 10 minutes
Cooking: 15 minutes

Asparagus and dippy eggs

Hollandaise sauce is the most delicious thing but it's quite a job to make. This cheat's version has the same wonderful flavours but takes almost no time. Basically you just add the classic hollandaise ingredients of butter and lemon juice to boiled eggs and dip your asparagus into the yummy buttery yolks. Deeply satisfying.

1 Put the asparagus in a steamer over a saucepan of boiling water and steam for 5 minutes or until tender, depending on the thickness of the stems. Remove and set aside. (If you don't have a steamer you could put the asparagus in a colander over a pan of boiling water and cover it with a lid.)

2 Meanwhile, bring another saucepan of water to the boil. Add the eggs and boil them for exactly 5 minutes.

3 Remove the eggs from the pan, place them in egg cups and cut off the tops. To each egg, add a squeeze of lemon juice, a dot of butter and a sprinkling of chopped chives. Serve immediately with the asparagus to dip into the egg yolk 'hollandaise'. Season to taste.

Serves 4

129 calories per serving

1 bunch of asparagus (about 250g)
4 large eggs
1 lemon
10g butter
1 tbsp chopped chives
salt and black pepper

Time check

Prep: 5 minutes
Cooking: 10 minutes

Baked eggs Florentine

I completely love eggs and this dish of eggs nestling on a mound of creamy spinach makes a perfect lunch for me. Protein, greens and a nice touch of cheesy flavour from the Parmesan – what more could you want?

1 Preheat the oven to 180°C/Fan 160°C/Gas 4. Lightly grease 4 ramekins with butter and set them aside.

2 Melt the butter in a large saucepan, add the onion and fry it over a medium heat until softened. Add the spinach, a few handfuls at a time, and let it wilt. Tip the spinach into a colander and squeeze out any excess liquid, then tip it back into the pan. Add the crème fraiche, then season well with freshly grated nutmeg, salt and pepper.

3 Divide the spinach mixture between the prepared ramekins. Make a dip in the middle of each and carefully crack in an egg, then scatter grated Parmesan over the top.

4 Place the dishes on a baking tray and bake for 15–20 minutes or until the egg whites are set but the yolks are still runny. Serve hot with some sourdough toast if you like.

Serves 4
298 calories per serving

15g butter, plus extra for greasing
1 onion, finely chopped
400g baby spinach
8 tbsp crème fraiche
grinding of fresh nutmeg
4 eggs
2 tbsp freshly grated Parmesan
   cheese
salt and black pepper

Time check

Prep: 10 minutes
Cooking: 15–20 minutes

Home-made pot noodles

These make an amazing take-to-work lunch. You can get everything ready in a couple of jars or containers in the morning, or the night before, then heat the stock when you want to eat and pour it into the jar of goodies. You can add whatever you like – prawns, chicken, thinly sliced peppers, baby corn, bean sprouts and so on – but do try to get good-quality fresh stock as it will really improve the flavour of the soup. If you want to make pots for the rest of the family, just multiply the ingredients accordingly.

1 Put the ginger, chilli, stock, soy sauce and sesame oil in a heatproof jar. Add a pinch of salt and a good grinding of black pepper and put the lid on the jar.

2 Place the vegetables and the prawns or chicken in a Kilner jar or a plastic sealable container. You need a container that will fit the stock in too, so make sure that it's big enough – it needs to hold about 500ml. Cook the noodles according to the packet instructions, then drain them, refresh in cold water and drain them again. Add the noodles to the container with the other ingredients.

3 When you are ready to eat, heat the stock and aromatics in a microwave or pour them into a pan and heat on the stove until piping hot. Pour the mixture over the noodles and vegetables and leave for a few minutes. Ready to eat straight away out of the jar.

Serves 1
331 calories

1 tsp grated fresh root ginger
1 tsp chopped red chilli
300ml fresh good-quality chicken stock
1 tsp dark soy sauce
2 tsp sesame oil
1 spring onion, sliced
4 sugar snap peas, halved lengthways
1 baby pak choi, shredded
½ carrot, cut into matchsticks
50g cooked king prawns or cooked chopped chicken breast
1 x 50g nest of uncooked wholegrain rice vermicelli noodles or glass noodles
salt and black pepper

Time check

Prep: 15 minutes
Cooking: 5 minutes

Nutty greens

You can use any greens you fancy for this, but just be sure to cook the more robust ones first and add the more delicate leaves, such as baby spinach, at the end. Stir-fry oil is a new discovery for me. You can find it in supermarkets and it has flavourings such as chilli and garlic already added so can save you a bit of time. You can also save time by using ready-cooked rice as suggested, but if you prefer to cook your own you'll need about 80g of raw rice.

1 Preheat the oven to 200°C/Fan 180°C/Gas 6. Spread the cashews on a baking tray and put them in the oven for 10 minutes or until they are light golden in colour. Remove them from the oven and set them aside.

2 Heat the oil in a wok, add the spring onions and fry them for 2 minutes. Add ginger and the garlic and chilli, if using, and fry for another minute. Then add the cabbage and the cavolo nero or kale with a splash of water and toss everything until the leaves are beginning to wilt slightly.

3 Heat the rice according to the packet instructions.

4 Scatter the toasted cashews and the sesame seeds over the greens and drizzle with the sesame oil. Serve immediately with the hot rice.

Davina's tips

You can also add some cooked chicken to this if you like – just cut down a little on the greens. BTW, you can buy sesame seeds already toasted – saves a bit of time. If you do want to toast your own, just toss the seeds in a dry pan over a medium heat for a few moments, stirring frequently. Keep a close eye on them so they don't burn.

Serves 4
375 calories per serving

100g cashew nuts
2 tbsp stir-fry oil
4 spring onions, chopped
20g fresh root ginger, peeled and cut into thin sticks
1 garlic clove, sliced (optional)
1 red chilli, deseeded and sliced (optional)
1 small spring cabbage, core removed and leaves thickly shredded
200g cavolo nero or kale, shredded
200g ready-cooked brown rice, to serve
2 tbsp toasted sesame seeds, to serve
1 tsp sesame oil, to serve

Time check

Prep: 15 minutes
Cooking: 15 minutes

Bean and chorizo soup

Full of flavour, this soup is really easy to put together and you have a lovely warming bowlful in no time. It's a great favourite in my house.

1 Put the chorizo in a large saucepan and fry it over a high heat for 2 minutes or until it's golden and crisp. Remove the chorizo from the pan, leaving the oil it has released, and set the chorizo aside.

2 Add the onion and peppers to the pan and season them with salt and pepper. Fry them in the chorizo oil over a medium heat for about 5 minutes or until softened. Add the harissa paste and garlic, then fry for another minute.

3 Put the chorizo back in the pan with the onion and peppers. Add the beans, chopped tomatoes and stock and bring it all to the boil. Turn down the heat, put a lid on the pan and leave the soup to simmer for 10 minutes.

4 To serve, ladle the soup into bowls and scatter with coriander leaves. Top with a swirl of chilli oil if you fancy.

Davina's tip

I find that the mini chorizos you find in the supermarket work really nicely here.

Serves 4

233 calories per serving

100g chorizo, cut into cubes
1 red onion, diced
2 peppers (red, yellow or orange), deseeded and diced
1 tbsp harissa paste
1 garlic clove, finely chopped
400g can of mixed beans, drained and rinsed
400g can of chopped tomatoes
600ml hot chicken or vegetable stock
small handful of coriander leaves or parsley, chopped
chilli oil, to garnish (optional)
salt and black pepper

Time check

Prep: 15 minutes
Cooking: 20 minutes

Roasted tomato and red pepper soup with goat cheese toasts

We grow loads of tomatoes in the summer and this is a great way to enjoy them. If you're buying tomatoes, look for really lovely deep red ones that are good and ripe for the best flavour. The goat cheese toasts are the perfect accompaniment.

1 Preheat the oven to 200°C/Fan 180°C/Gas 6. Put the tomatoes, peppers, onion and garlic on a large shallow roasting tray. Drizzle them with olive oil, scatter over the thyme and season well with salt and pepper. Roast the vegetables for 30 minutes or until tender and slightly charred, shaking the tray occasionally to make sure everything cooks evenly. Remove the tray from the oven and set the veg aside to cool for 5 minutes.

2 While the vegetables are roasting, drizzle the slices of bread with olive oil and toast them on a griddle pan for 1–2 minutes on each side until lightly charred. Whip together the goat cheese, cream, parsley and basil until smooth and season with salt and pepper. Spread this mixture over the toasts and scatter some thyme leaves on top.

4 When the garlic is cool enough to handle, squeeze the flesh out of the skins into the roasting tray and discard the skins. Tip the contents of the roasting tray into a saucepan, add the hot stock and blitz with a stick blender until smooth. If you don't have a stick blender, let the soup cool slightly, then blend it in a food processor or blender and tip it back into the pan. Add a little water if the soup seems too thick and warm through if necessary.

5 Serve the soup in bowls with the warm toasts.

Serves 4

126 calories per serving
300 calories per serving
(with goat cheese toasts)

1 kg ripe red tomatoes, quartered
2 red peppers, deseeded and roughly
  chopped
1 red onion, chopped
3 garlic cloves, unpeeled
2 tbsp olive oil
3 sprigs of fresh thyme
200–300ml hot chicken or vegetable
  stock
salt and black pepper

Goat cheese toasts
4 slices of soda or sourdough bread
olive oil, for drizzling
50g soft goat cheese
1 tsp single cream
1 tbsp finely chopped parsley and
  basil
2 sprigs of thyme, leaves only

Time check

Prep: 15 minutes
Cooking: 35 minutes

Minty pea soup

Mmmm – the colour of this is ridiculous! The soup is great hot but also perfect served chilled on a summer's day. Lovely with a dollop of crème fraiche and a few mint leaves or try adding a swirl of mint oil, which looks pretty and very posh.

1 Heat the oil in a large saucepan. Add the leek and onion and cook them over a gentle heat for 5 minutes or until the onion is soft but not coloured. Add the garlic and cook for a further minute.

2 Add 400g of the peas, the lettuce, most of the mint leaves (reserving some for garnishing later) and 700ml of the stock. Bring the soup to the boil and then simmer it for 2–3 minutes.

3 Blend the soup with a stick blender or in a food processor until you have a thick purée. Add more stock to get the consistency you like, then add the remaining peas and warm though for a further 2–3 minutes. Add lemon juice and seasoning to taste.

4 Serve the soup hot or cold, with a drizzle of crème fraiche and/or a swirl of mint oil and a scattering of chopped mint. Delicious served with some crusty soda or sourdough bread.

Davina's tip

To make the mint oil, blitz a large handful of fresh mint leaves with 2–3 tablespoons of olive oil in a small blender until smooth, then season with salt and pepper. Add more oil if necessary to make a pourable consistency.

Serves 4

216 calories per serving

1 tbsp olive oil
1 medium leek trimmed and
    roughly chopped
1 onion, roughly chopped
1 garlic clove, finely chopped
500g frozen peas
1 baby gem lettuce, root trimmed and
    leaves roughly chopped
large handful of fresh mint leaves
800ml hot chicken or vegetable stock
1–2 tbsp lemon juice
4 tbsp crème fraiche, to serve
    (optional)
salt and black pepper

Time check

Prep: 10 minutes
Cooking: 15 minutes

Sunshine soup

Just looking at this soup makes me happy – and that's even before I taste a spoonful. You don't have to make the seed sprinkle topping, but it is surprisingly scrumptious and adds extra goodness.

1 Preheat the oven to 200°C/Fan 180°C/Gas 6. Put the squash, carrots, onion and garlic in a large roasting tin. Drizzle them with olive oil, season well and scatter over the chilli flakes, if using, and the rosemary or thyme. Roast the vegetables for 30 minutes or until golden, tender and slightly charred, turning them occasionally with tongs to make sure they cook evenly.

2 Once the vegetables are tender, tip them into a large saucepan. Squeeze the garlic flesh out of the skins into the saucepan and discard the skins. Strip the leaves off the rosemary or thyme stalks and add them to the pan.

3 Add the orange juice and stock and blend the soup with a stick blender until completely smooth. If you don't have a stick blender, let the soup cool slightly, then blitz it in a food processor or blender and tip it back into the pan.

4 For the seed sprinkle topping, add the sesame oil and seeds to a small frying pan and toast over a medium heat for 1–2 minutes. Add the soy sauce and chilli flakes, if using, and toss to coat.

5 Reheat the soup if necessary, then ladle it into bowls. Top with a drizzle of oil and a scattering of the toasted seeds.

Serves 4
337 calories per serving
(including seed topping)

1 butternut squash, seeds removed, cut into 3cm chunks (about 1kg)
3 carrots, cut into 3cm chunks
1 onion, roughly chopped
2 garlic cloves, unpeeled
2 tbsp olive oil, plus extra to garnish
pinch of chilli flakes (optional)
2 sprigs of rosemary or thyme
juice of ½ orange
900ml hot chicken or vegetable stock
salt and black pepper

Seed sprinkle topping
1 tbsp sesame oil
3 tbsp pumpkin seeds
1 tsp soy sauce
pinch of chilli flakes (optional)

Time check

Prep: 10 minutes
Cooking: 35 minutes

Supergreen soup

Supergreen and super healthy – I love this soup and I like to add a mixture of different greens to make it fabulously nourishing. You can feel it doing you good and happily the zingy Asian flavours make it taste great too.

1 Heat the oil in a large saucepan. Add the spring onions and fry them over a gentle heat for about 5 minutes or until softened but not coloured. Add the chilli (reserving a little for the garnish), the garlic, ginger and turmeric, then season with salt and pepper and fry for another 2 minutes.

2 Add the broccoli and stock to the pan. Bring the stock to the boil and simmer it for 3 minutes. Add the rest of the greens and simmer for another 2 minutes or until the leaves have wilted.

3 Stir in the coconut milk (reserving 2 tablespoons for the garnish), then blitz the soup with a stick blender until it is completely smooth. Add a little lime zest and juice to taste and check the seasoning.

4 Warm the soup through if necessary, then pour it into bowls. Add a swirl of coconut milk to each serving, then scatter with the reserved green chilli and the chopped coriander and red chilli.

Serves 4

156 calories per serving

1 tbsp stir-fry oil
1 bunch of spring onions, sliced
1 green chilli, deseeded and sliced
2 garlic cloves, chopped
15g fresh root ginger, peeled and
    finely chopped
1 tsp ground turmeric
100g broccoli, cut into florets
750ml hot chicken or vegetable stock
350g greens, such as baby spinach
    and kale
200ml coconut milk, plus extra for
    serving
finely grated zest of 1 lime, plus a
    squeeze of juice
2 tbsp chopped coriander, to serve
½ red chilli, deseeded and chopped,
    to serve
salt and black pepper

Time check

Prep: 15 minutes
Cooking: 15 minutes

Beetroot and apple soup

You need the vac packs of cooked beetroot for this – not the kind with vinegar! Once you have those, the rest is a breeze and the soup is on the table in less than half an hour. And beetroot is soooo good for you – full of vitamins and minerals – as well as being mega delicious and naturally sweet. It really hits the spot.

1 Heat the olive oil in a large saucepan, add the onion and fry it for 5 minutes or until softened. Add the garlic and thyme and fry for another minute.

2 Set aside 50g each of the beetroot and apples for garnishing the soup and add the rest to the pan. Add the hot stock and bring it to the boil, then simmer for 10 minutes or until the apples are tender.

3 Remove the pan from the heat and blend the soup with a stick blender until it is smooth and has the consistency you like. Season it well. If you don't have a stick blender, let the soup cool slightly, then blitz it in a food processor or blender and tip it back into the pan. Warm the soup through if necessary.

4 Finely dice the reserved beetroot and apple. Ladle the soup into bowls, drizzle a teaspoon of soured cream over each serving, then scatter with the reserved chopped beetroot and apple. Sprinkle some thyme leaves over the top.

Davina's tip

This soup freezes well so you might like to make double the quantity and store some for another day. Just let it cool completely, then tip it into a freezer-proof container and stash it away for up to 3 months. To serve, defrost fully and heat to boiling point.

Serves 4

172 calories per serving

1 tbsp olive oil
1 red onion, roughly chopped
1 garlic clove, sliced
2 sprigs of fresh thyme, plus extra
    for serving
2 x 300g packs of cooked beetroot,
    drained and chopped into cubes
2 apples, cored and chopped
800ml–1 litre hot chicken or vegetable
    stock
4 tsp soured cream, to serve
salt and black pepper

Time check

Prep: 10 minutes
Cooking: 15 minutes

Cold tomato soup à la AJ

This is my friend AJ's very special recipe for a gazpacho-style soup which is amazing. Everyone loves it and AJ is asked to bring some along to every summer party and picnic. Thank you AJ!

1 Place all the ingredients for the soup in a large bowl, reserving half the basil and coriander for later. There's no need to skin or deseed the tomatoes or to deseed the cucumber. Mix well, then cover and leave the soup in the fridge overnight for the flavours to intensify.

2 When you want to serve the soup, use a hand blender to blitz the ingredients or whiz it in a blender in batches. If you have the time or inclination, push the soup through a sieve.

3 Cut or tear the sourdough into small cubes and fry them in olive oil with a little salt and pepper until crisp and golden. Drain them on kitchen paper and set aside.

4 Serve the soup in bowls or glasses and drizzle with a little extra virgin olive oil and scatter with the reserved herbs before serving. You could also cut the other pepper halves into small cubes and scatter these over the soup if you like.

Davina's tip

This makes a very smooth soup, but if you want chunky - just skip the sieving stage.

Serves 4

227 calories per serving

6 ripe tomatoes (preferably plum or vine), chopped
½ cucumber, peeled and chopped
½ red pepper, deseeded and chopped
½ green pepper, deseeded and chopped
1 garlic clove, finely chopped
1–2 tbsp Worcestershire sauce
75ml extra virgin olive oil, plus extra for serving
6 drops of Tabasco Chipotle
50ml Chianti red wine vinegar
200ml good-quality tomato juice
½ tsp sea salt flakes
½ tsp crushed black peppercorns
small handful of basil leaves, shredded
small handful of coriander, chopped

Croutons

2 slices of sourdough bread
1 tbsp olive oil
salt and black pepper

Time check

Prep: 15 minutes
Cooking: 5 minutes

—2—

speedy salads

Halloumi and asparagus salad 47
Grilled corn, avocado and feta salad 48
Broccoli, spelt and orange salad 51
Courgette and shrimp salad 52
Cucumber noodle, chicken and cashew salad 55
Chicken, carrot and chickpea salad 56
Roasted beetroot and celeriac salad 59
Butternut and couscous salad 60
Spicy prawn or chicken salad 63

Halloumi and asparagus salad

I love, love, love edamame beans – young soy beans – and now I've discovered I can buy packs of frozen ones I love them even more. One thing – it's best to serve this as soon as the halloumi cheese is cooked as it turns bouncy very quickly when it cools and that's not so nice.

1 First make the dressing. Heat the oil in a saucepan and add the garlic, cherry tomatoes and sun-dried tomatoes. Toss them over a high heat for a minute or until the tomatoes have softened slightly. Add the sherry vinegar and season to taste, then scatter over the basil and set aside.

2 Pop the edamame beans into a pan of boiling water and bring the water back to the boil. Drain the beans, then rinse them in cold water and set them aside.

3 Heat a griddle pan until it's smoking hot. Toss the asparagus in a little of the oil, then griddle it for 3–4 minutes or until lightly charred and just tender. Set aside. Brush the slices of halloumi with the rest of the oil and griddle for a minute on each side.

4 Divide the watercress between 4 plates, top with the asparagus, halloumi and edamame beans. Pour over the tomato dressing and serve immediately.

Serves 4
380 calories per serving

100g edamame beans
300g pack of asparagus tips
2 tbsp olive oil
1 x 200g pack of halloumi, sliced
90g watercress
salt and black pepper

Tomato dressing
3 tbsp olive oil
1 garlic clove, chopped
200g cherry tomatoes, halved
    (a mix of colours is good)
40g sun-dried tomatoes, chopped
2 tsp sherry vinegar
small handful of basil leaves

Time check

Prep: 10 minutes
Cooking: 10 minutes

Grilled corn, avocado and feta salad

A rainbow in a bowl! The grilled corn gives this salad a fab flavour and if you happen to have the barbecue on the go and you can cook the corn on that – even better. The tiny touch of honey does balance the dressing nicely, but feel free to leave it out if you're going sugar free.

1 Preheat the grill to high. Brush the corn cobs with oil and season them well. Grill the cobs for 15–20 minutes or until lightly charred and tender, turning them occasionally.

2 Remove the corn cobs from the grill and leave them to cool for a couple of minutes. When they're cool enough to handle, remove the kernels with a sharp knife.

3 Put the lettuce leaves in a serving bowl, top with the roasted corn and add the avocado, peppers, tomatoes and feta.

4 For the dressing, mix together the lime zest and juice with the oil, chilli, coriander and the honey, if using, in a small jug, then season well. Pour the dressing over the salad and toss before serving.

Serves 4
281 calories per serving

2 corn cobs, outer leaves and husk removed
1 tbsp olive oil
2 little gem lettuces, leaves separated
1 ripe avocado, stone removed and flesh chopped
2 ready-roasted peppers from a jar, rinsed, drained and cut into strips
2 medium tomatoes, cut into quarters
100g feta cheese, crumbled
salt and black pepper

Dressing
finely grated zest and juice of 1 lime
3 tbsp olive oil
½ red chilli, deseeded and finely chopped (or more if you like it spicy)
small handful of coriander leaves, chopped
1 tsp runny honey (optional)

Time check
Prep: 15 minutes
Cooking: 20 minutes

Broccoli, spelt and orange salad

A bit of citrus in a salad perks it up beautifully and gives it a lovely tangy flavour. I use a pack of ready-cooked spelt for speed, but you can, of course, cook your own if you prefer or use any other smart carbs you like, such as cooked quinoa, pearl barley, brown rice or barley couscous. So yummy.

1 Heat up the spelt according to the packet instructions and tip it into a serving bowl.

2 Put the broccoli in a steamer or a colander over a pan of boiling water and steam for 2 minutes, then set it aside. Heat the olive oil in a large frying pan, add the broccoli and cook it gently for 2–3 minutes. Add the chilli and garlic and fry for another minute.

3 To make the dressing, whisk together the tahini, sesame oil, juice of half an orange and the rice vinegar in a small jug and season with salt and black pepper. Peel and segment the remaining oranges, discarding the pith.

4 Mix the sautéed broccoli with the cooked spelt and add the orange segments. Pour over the dressing, scatter with sesame seeds and serve.

Serves 4

354 calories per serving

300g ready-cooked spelt
300g tenderstem or purple
    sprouting broccoli
1 tbsp olive oil
1 red chilli, deseeded and sliced
2 garlic cloves, finely sliced
2 tbsp sesame seeds, to garnish

Dressing
1 tbsp tahini
2 tbsp sesame oil
2 oranges
1 tsp rice vinegar
salt and black pepper

Time check

Prep: 10 minutes
Cooking: 10 minutes

Courgette and shrimp salad

Brown shrimps are delish in this and have a lovely sweet taste, but cooked king prawns work well too. Do allow time to let the salad sit and marinate in the dressing for 20 minutes if poss, but add the rocket just before serving or it will wilt too much. No one likes a soggy leaf . . .

1 Slice the courgettes lengthways into thin ribbons using a vegetable peeler or a mandolin – use the middles in another dish if they are too difficult to cut into ribbons. Place the ribbons in a large bowl.

2 Mix the lemon juice and zest in a bowl with the olive oil, chopped mint, capers and shrimps or prawns, then season with salt and pepper. Pour this mixture over the courgette ribbons. Toss everything together, then cover and set aside for 20 minutes if you have time, so that the courgette ribbons have a chance to soften slightly and take on the flavours of the dressing.

3 Add the rocket, toss again and serve.

Serves 4
130 calories per serving

2 medium courgettes
juice and finely grated zest
    of ½ lemon
3 tbsp olive oil
3 tbsp chopped fresh mint leaves
2 tbsp capers, rinsed and drained
150g brown shrimps or 200g cooked
    king prawns
100g wild rocket leaves
salt and black pepper

Time check

Prep: 10 minutes, plus
    marinating time
Cooking: 0 minutes

Cucumber noodle, chicken and cashew salad

Smoked chicken is easy to find in supermarkets now and adds a lovely depth of flavour, but you can use ordinary cooked chicken instead if you like. This is great to eat at home and it travels well too. You can pack it into a box to take to work with you. I love a speedy salad!

1 Preheat the oven to 200°C/Fan 180°C/Gas 6. Place the cashews on a baking tray and toast them for 5 minutes or until light golden. Remove them from the oven and leave them to cool.

2 Cut the cucumbers into long ribbons, using a spiraliser if you have one, then cut the ribbons into 3 (so they are easier to eat). If you don't have a spiraliser, use a vegetable peeler. Put the ribbons in a large bowl and add the smoked chicken, sunblush tomatoes and cashew nuts.

3 Mix together the honey, if using, with the lime juice and zest, chilli and oils in a jug. Add most of the herbs, keeping the smallest leaves for garnishing. Season the dressing, then pour it over the salad. Garnish with the reserved leaves and serve.

Davina's tip

If you're making this recipe to take to work as a packed lunch, put the salad in a sealable container and the dressing in a separate pot. Dress the salad just before eating.

Serves 4

334 calories per serving

100g unsalted cashew nuts
2 cucumbers
200g smoked chicken, shredded
75g sunblush tomatoes, chopped

Herb dressing

1 tsp runny honey (optional)
juice and finely grated zest of 1 lime
1 red chilli, deseeded and finely
    chopped
1 tbsp sesame oil
2 tbsp extra virgin olive oil
small handful each of fresh basil
    and coriander leaves
salt and black pepper

Time check

Prep: 15 minutes
Cooking: 5 minutes

Chicken, carrot and chickpea salad

This is a great salad for a packed lunch, as it can be made and stored in the fridge for up to two days. For a change, you could also use smoked duck or cooked king prawns instead of chicken. There's no cooking needed here – got to love that every now and again.

1 Put the grated carrot in a large bowl. Add the chickpeas, sultanas, mint and chicken.

2 Mix together the orange juice and zest, olive oil and harissa in a small jug and season with salt and pepper. Pour the dressing over the salad and mix well. If you have time, cover the salad and leave it in the fridge for an hour for the flavour to develop.

Serves 4

342 calories per serving

3 carrots, coarsely grated
400g can of chickpeas, drained
    and rinsed
60g sultanas
4 tbsp chopped fresh mint leaves
250g smoked chicken or cooked
    chicken breast, shredded

Dressing

juice and finely grated zest of
    1 orange
3 tbsp olive oil
1 tbsp harissa (or more if you like)
salt and black pepper

Time check

Prep: 15 minutes
Cooking: 0 minutes

Roasted beetroot and celeriac salad

This is a really hearty, satisfying salad and it looks so colourful with the red beetroot and pomegranate seeds. Use ready-cooked quinoa for speed – let's make things easy on ourselves – but cook your own if you have the time.

1 Preheat the oven to 200°C/Fan 180°C/Gas 6. Put the red onion and celeriac in a large shallow roasting tin and drizzle with a tablespoon of the olive oil. Season the vegetables with salt and pepper, then pop them in the oven to roast for 15 minutes.

2 Add the beetroot and a tablespoon of the pomegranate molasses and roast for another 15 minutes.

3 If using ready-cooked quinoa, warm it up according to the packet instructions and tip it into a bowl.

4 Tip the roasted vegetables on top of the quinoa and scatter over the cheese, pomegranate seeds and parsley or mint. Add the rest of the pomegranate molasses and olive oil and season well.

Davina's tip

If you have time to cook your own quinoa, you'll need about 75g. Rinse it well, then put it in a saucepan and toast it for a couple of minutes. Add 200ml of water or stock and season with salt. Bring to the boil, then turn the heat down to a simmer, cover the pan and cook for 15 minutes. By this time all the water should be absorbed. Remove from the heat and leave to stand for 5 minutes before using.

Serves 4

283 calories per serving

1 red onion, cut into cubes or wedges
½ celeriac, cut into cubes
3 tbsp olive oil
300g pack of cooked beetroot, drained and cut into wedges
3 tbsp pomegranate molasses
250g ready-cooked mixed colour quinoa
50g hard goat cheese, crumbled
30g pomegranate seeds
2 tbsp chopped parsley or mint
salt and black pepper

Time check

Prep: 15 minutes
Cooking: 30 minutes

Butternut and couscous salad

For speed's sake you can cook the squash with the peel on, but remove it if you prefer – it tastes good either way. This is a lovely comforting dish and the bright colour is just what you need on chilly grey day. It's nice served warm or cold.

1 Preheat the oven to 200°C/Fan 180°C/Gas 6. Top and tail the butternut squash and cut it in half. Remove the seeds, then cut the squash into long wedges and put them in a roasting tin with the onion. Drizzle the veggies with some of the oil, scatter over the cinnamon and paprika and season well. Roast for 30 minutes or until the squash and onion wedges are tender and slightly charred, turning the squash halfway through.

2 Meanwhile, put the couscous in a heatproof bowl and pour over enough of the hot stock to just cover it. Add the rest of the oil and the lemon zest. Cover the bowl with cling film and set the couscous aside for 5 minutes or until it has absorbed all the stock. Fluff it up with a fork and then stir in the lemon juice and half the chopped mint.

3 Toast the pumpkin seeds in a dry frying pan over a low heat for about 2 minutes or until crisp and lightly golden.

4 Tip the couscous on to a serving dish and top with the roasted squash. Mix the chilli sauce with the yoghurt in a small jug, then pour this over the salad. Scatter over the pumpkin seeds and the rest of the chopped mint and serve.

Davina's tip

If you make this for a packed lunch, put the dressing in a separate container and pour it over the salad when you're ready to eat.

Serves 4
508 calories per serving

1 butternut squash
1 red onion, cut into wedges
2 tbsp olive oil
½ tsp ground cinnamon
1 tsp paprika
200g barley couscous
200ml hot chicken or vegetable stock
finely grated zest and juice of 1 lemon
small handful of mint leaves, chopped
30g pumpkin seeds
2 tsp chilli sauce (sriracha is good)
150g plain yoghurt
salt and black pepper

Time check

Prep: 15 minutes
Cooking: 30 minutes

Spicy prawn or chicken salad

This tasty salad has the gorgeous Thai flavours that I love. It looks good and it does you good and it's great for a take-to-work lunch or as part of a summer lunch buffet. You can spiralise the carrot and cucumber if you're into spiralising. I am, and so are the kids.

1 For the dressing, whisk together the lime juice, fish sauce, mirin, honey, sesame oil and chilli in a small bowl and season with salt and pepper.

2 Put the peanuts, if using, in a dry frying pan and toast them over a low heat for 5 minutes or until golden. Set them aside to cool, then chop them roughly.

3 Place the rest of the ingredients in a serving bowl, keeping back a few herbs and the peanuts, then add the prawns or chicken. Pour the dressing over the salad and scatter the remaining herbs and the peanuts, if using, over the top before serving.

Serves 4

173 calories per serving
(with prawns)
196 calories per serving
(with chicken)

30g unsalted peanuts (optional)
1 little gem lettuce, finely shredded
100g bean sprouts
1 large carrot, finely shredded
½ cucumber, quartered lengthways, deseeded and finely sliced
½ red pepper, deseeded and finely sliced
small handful each of fresh mint and coriander leaves
200g cooked king prawns or 150g cooked chicken breast, thinly sliced

Dressing
4 tbsp fresh lime juice
3 tsp fish sauce (nam pla)
1 tbsp mirin
1 tsp runny honey
2 tbsp sesame oil
1 red chilli, deseeded and finely chopped
salt and black pepper

Time check

Prep: 15 minutes
Cooking: 5 minutes

—3—

Easy Suppers

Baked roasted tomato risotto 67

Stuffed courgettes 68

Cauliflower 'steaks' with onion and chorizo 71

Spaghetti with creamy veggie sauce 72

Cod and pesto parcels 75

Pan-fried lemon sole with hot tomato salsa 76

Glazed salmon with rainbow vegetables 79

Smoked mackerel salad with apple dressing 80

Salmon and sweet potato fishcakes 83

Grilled tuna with peppers and lentils 84

Crunchy buttermilk chicken with roasted ratatouille 87

Chicken Caesar salad 88

Lamb and apricot pilaf 91

Pork fillet with mushroom sauce 92

Squash 'spaghetti' with pancetta sauce 95

Seared steak with five-bean salad 96

Baked roasted tomato risotto

I do love a risotto – one of the most comforting of all suppers – but sometimes I don't have time to stand over the stove stirring for 20 minutes. So this baked version is a real find – just pop it in the oven and leave it to cook. I like to use a three-grain mixture containing rice, spelt and barley, which gives a lovely texture, but use brown risotto rice if you prefer – check the cooking time though, as it might take a bit longer.

1 Preheat the oven to 200°C/Fan 180°C/Gas 6. Place the tomatoes on a baking tray and drizzle a tablespoon of the olive oil over them. Add 2 sprigs of rosemary, season well, then roast the tomatoes for 10 minutes or until softened and slightly charred.

2 Meanwhile, heat the rest of the olive oil in a flameproof casserole dish, add the onion, celery and garlic, then fry them for 5 minutes. Add the rice and stir to coat all the grains, then pour in the wine and let it bubble for 2–3 minutes.

3 Pour the hot stock over the rice and add the roasted tomatoes – discarding the rosemary. Finely chop the remaining rosemary leaves and stir them in. Put the lid on the casserole dish, place it in the oven and bake the risotto for 18 minutes or until the rice is tender.

4 Just before serving, stir in the spinach, mascarpone and Parmesan and stir until the spinach is wilted. Taste and add more salt and pepper if necessary, then serve with extra Parmesan cheese.

Davina's tip

If you don't have any mascarpone, you can use a couple of good knobs of butter instead.

Serves 4
460 calories per serving

300g cherry tomatoes, halved
    (mix of colours is nice)
3 tbsp olive oil
3 sprigs of rosemary
1 onion, finely chopped
2 celery sticks, finely chopped
2 garlic cloves, finely chopped
300g three-grain risotto rice
100ml white wine
700ml hot chicken or vegetable stock
100g baby spinach
2 tbsp mascarpone
2 tbsp finely grated Parmesan cheese,
    plus extra for serving
salt and black pepper

Time check

Prep: 15 minutes
Cooking: 30 minutes

Stuffed courgettes

My kids call these courgette canoes – they're little boatloads of goodies! This is a great dish for preparing ahead, then you can pop it in the oven for 10 minutes when you're ready to eat. I've suggested ready-cooked brown rice to save time but you can cook your own if you prefer.

1 Preheat the oven to 220°C/Fan 200°C/Gas 7. Scoop out some flesh from the middle of each courgette with a teaspoon, then finely chop the flesh and set it aside.

2 Place the courgettes cut-side up in a single layer in a shallow roasting tray. Drizzle them with a little oil and bake for 20 minutes.

3 Meanwhile, fry the onion in a tablespoon of the oil for 5 minutes or until softened. Add the pine nuts, garlic and chopped courgette, season well and fry for another 1–2 minutes. Add the chopped apricots, rice and herbs and check the seasoning.

4 Spoon the mixture into the courgette halves and scatter with Parmesan or feta. Drizzle with a little more oil and bake for 10 minutes or until the courgettes are softened and the topping is golden and crisp. Serve hot with a large green salad.

Serves 4

330 calories per serving

4 medium courgettes, halved
    lengthways
2 tbsp olive oil
1 red onion, finely chopped
50g pine nuts
2 garlic cloves, finely chopped
75g dried apricots, chopped
300g ready-cooked brown rice
3 tbsp chopped fresh herbs, such as
    parsley or thyme
2 tbsp grated Parmesan cheese or
    40g feta cheese, crumbled
salt and black pepper

Time check

Prep: 20 minutes
Cooking: 35 minutes

Cauliflower 'steaks' with onion and chorizo

This is a great way of cooking cauliflower and although it's not a vegetarian dish because of the chorizo, it still gives a good boost to your five a day. If you're not a chorizo lover you could use little cubes of pancetta. And if you want to be a bit more exotic you could try cavolo nero instead of spinach – it's a type of Italian cabbage and the leaves have more body than spinach and a good strong flavour.

1 Preheat the oven to 200°C/Fan 180°C/Gas 6. Cutting through the centre of the cauliflower, slice it into 4 x 2cm-thick 'steaks'. Pop the rest of the cauliflower into a food bag and use it in another dish.

2 Heat a tablespoon of the oil in a large frying pan. Add 2 of the steaks and fry them for 2–3 minutes on each side or until golden. Remove them from the pan and place them on a baking tray, then cook the other 2 cauli 'steaks' and place them on the baking tray. Put the baking tray in the oven and roast the cauliflower for 10 minutes or until tender.

3 Meanwhile, add the chorizo to the pan and fry it for 2–3 minutes or until golden. Remove the chorizo from the pan and set it aside. Wipe out the pan with kitchen paper.

4 Pour the rest of the oil into the frying pan and add the sliced onion. Fry the onion over a medium heat for 10 minutes or until it's softened and beginning to caramelise. Add the garlic and fry for another minute. Then add the spinach or cavolo nero and allow the leaves to wilt for 1–2 minutes. Add the cooked chorizo, scatter over the lemon zest and a squeeze of lemon juice and season well.

5 To serve, divide the greens and chorizo mixture between 4 plates and add the cauli 'steaks'. Serve at once.

Serves 4
285 calories per serving

1 large cauliflower
3 tbsp olive oil
100g chorizo, cut into cubes
1 red onion, thinly sliced
2 garlic cloves, finely chopped
300g spinach or 150g cavolo nero
finely grated zest of ½ lemon and
    a squeeze of juice
salt and black pepper

Time check

Prep: 15 minutes
Cooking: 20 minutes

Spaghetti with creamy veggie sauce

This is a super-quick supper that all the family will enjoy. My kids weren't keen on brown pasta at first, but now they prefer it. And I've found that even children who are a bit suspicious of green things love this one – and so do I.

1 Cook the spaghetti in boiling salted water according to the packet instructions and drain. Toss it with a little of the olive oil.

2 Meanwhile, heat the rest of the olive oil in a separate pan. Add the leeks, season them well and fry them gently over a medium heat for 5 minutes until softened, stirring occasionally. Add 2 tablespoons of water to help the leeks steam and cook. Once all the water has evaporated from the pan, add the garlic and fry it for a minute.

3 Add the courgette and fry it for 2–3 minutes, then stir in the crème fraiche, grated Parmesan and chopped basil. Taste and season with salt and pepper as needed.

4 Divide the spaghetti between 4 plates, top with the sauce and scatter over some extra Parmesan and basil leaves before serving.

Serves 4
375 calories per serving

200g wholewheat spaghetti
2 tbsp olive oil
2 leeks, finely sliced
2 garlic cloves, finely chopped
1 large courgette, grated
150ml crème fraiche
20g Parmesan cheese, grated, plus
    extra to serve
small handful of basil leaves,
    chopped, plus some to garnish
salt and black pepper

Time check

Prep: 10 minutes
Cooking: 10 minutes

Cod and pesto parcels

My perfect food when I'm in a hurry. These are so quick to make and everyone loves them – it's a really easy way of cooking and serving fish. Fresh pesto from the deli counter is fine or you can make your own; it's easy – have a look at my recipe below. You can use a mixture of the green veg I've suggested or just a couple of kinds, but I do find I have to cook the green beans briefly first to make sure they are tender enough. The others all cook beautifully in the parcels.

1 Preheat the oven to 200°C/Fan 180°C/Gas 6. Cut out 4 x 40cm squares of baking paper and the same of foil. Lay the paper squares on top of the foil squares and brush them lightly with a little olive oil.

2 Blanch the green beans in a saucepan of boiling, salted water for 2 minutes. Drain them and rinse in cold water to stop them cooking, then mix them with the other vegetables.

3 Divide the vegetables between the 4 squares, add a cod fillet to each and season well. Add a tablespoon of pesto on top of each fillet, then drizzle with a little olive oil. Scatter the cherry tomatoes around the vegetables and add 2 wedges of lemon to each parcel. Scrunch up the paper and foil, making sure you leave a little space around the fish.

4 Place the parcels on a baking tray and bake them for 15–20 minutes or until the fish is just cooked through and the vegetables are tender. Serve the parcels at the table so everyone can enjoy opening their own. Good with some steamed brown rice.

Davina's tip

I always used to buy pesto but I've discovered how easy it is to make. Just put a small clove of garlic, 2 tablespoons of toasted pine nuts and a large handful of fresh basil leaves in a blender with 2 tablespoons of olive oil and a tablespoon of grated Parmesan cheese. Season with salt and pepper and blend until smooth. Wow!

Serves 4

265 calories per serving

2 tbsp olive oil
400g mix of green beans, mangetout, tenderstem broccoli or sugar snap peas
4 x 150–175g cod fillets, skinned
4 tbsp fresh pesto
250g cherry tomatoes, halved
1 lemon, cut into wedges
salt and black pepper

Time check

Prep: 10 minutes
Cooking: 20 minutes

Pan-fried lemon sole with hot tomato salsa

Lemon sole is easy to cook and much cheaper than Dover sole, and I love this punchy salsa, which works so well with the fish and its lemony buttery juices. Some fine green beans are good on the side.

1 First make the salsa. Heat the olive oil in a large frying pan, add the red onion and fry it over a medium heat until softened but not coloured. Add the chilli and garlic and fry for another minute. Stir in the chopped tomatoes and olives and warm them through for a minute or so. Remove the pan from the heat, stir in the basil and season well. Keep the sauce warm while you cook the fish.

2 Spread the flour on a plate and season it with salt and pepper. Dust the lemon sole fillets in the flour and shake off the excess.

3 Heat the olive oil in a large frying pan, add a couple of sole fillets and fry them for 2 minutes on one side, then turn them over and fry for another 2 minutes or until just cooked. Remove the fillets from the pan and set them aside while you cook the rest.

4 Melt the butter in the pan and add the lemon juice. Put the fish back in the pan and baste it with the lemony buttery juices.

5 Serve the fish with the pan juices and the tomato salsa.

Davina's tip

The salsa is also delicious served with wholemeal penne pasta and grated Parmesan.

Serves 4
386 calories per serving

2 tbsp wholemeal spelt flour
4 double lemon sole fillets
2 tbsp olive oil
15g butter
juice of 1 lemon
salt and black pepper

Hot tomato salsa
2 tbsp olive oil
1 red onion, finely chopped
½ long red chilli, deseeded and finely
    chopped
2 garlic cloves, finely chopped
200g red and yellow cherry tomatoes,
    quartered
50g pitted Kalamata olives, chopped
small handful of fresh basil leaves,
    shredded

Time check

Prep: 10 minutes
Cooking: 10 minutes

Glazed salmon with rainbow vegetables

This is so speedy and incredibly yummy. The spiralised carrot and courgette make it seem like you're having a lovely noodly stir-fry – but without the carbs! I was a bit worried about the miso paste at first, but you can find it in supermarkets alongside the mirin and soy sauce and it's cheap, tasty and easy to use. And I love stir-fry oil which adds flavour and reduces hassle.

1 Preheat the oven to 200°C/Fan 180°C/Gas 6. Mix the mirin, sesame oil, soy sauce and miso together in a bowl.

2 Place the salmon fillets in a shallow roasting tray and pour over a few tablespoons of the miso mixture over them (reserve the rest for later). Scatter the spring onions and sesame seeds over the top, season and then bake in the oven for 8–10 minutes.

3 Meanwhile, cook the vegetables. Heat the stir-fry oil and sesame oil in a wok. Add the peppers and spiralised carrot and fry for 2 minutes. Add the ginger and fry for another minute, then add the courgette and pak choi and fry for 1–2 minutes more. Pour over the remaining miso mixture and let everything bubble for 1 minute.

4 Divide the vegetables between 4 plates and top with the salmon and pan juices. Sprinkle with extra sesame seeds and serve at once.

Serves 4
516 calories per serving

2 tbsp mirin
1 tbsp sesame oil
2 tbsp soy sauce
1 tbsp miso paste
4 x 150g salmon fillets, skinned
2 spring onions, finely sliced
2 tbsp sesame seeds, plus extra to
    serve
salt and black pepper

Rainbow vegetables
2 tbsp stir-fry oil
1 tsp sesame oil
1 red and yellow pepper, deseeded
    and thinly sliced
1 large carrot, spiralised
15g fresh root ginger, cut into thin
    matchsticks
1 courgette, spiralised
300g baby pak choi, leaves chopped

Time check

Prep: 15 minutes
Cooking: 15 minutes

Smoked mackerel salad with apple dressing

Smoked mackerel is a great standby for an easy, nourishing supper and you can buy it in any supermarket these days. It works beautifully with the roast squash. Walnut oil is perfect in the dressing if you happen to have some, but otherwise it's fine to use olive oil.

1 Preheat the oven to 200°C/Fan 180°C/Gas 6. Put the cubes of squash on a shallow baking tray, spacing them well apart. Drizzle them with olive oil, sprinkle with thyme and season well. Roast the squash for 25 minutes until it's tender and golden, then scatter in the walnut halves and roast for another 5 minutes.

2 To make the dressing, grate the apple into a bowl, then add the oil, cider vinegar and seasoning.

3 Divide the lamb's lettuce between 4 plates and top with the roasted squash, walnuts and tray juices. Scatter over the pieces of smoked mackerel, then pour over the apple dressing and serve immediately.

Serves 4
517 calories per serving

600g butternut squash, cut into cubes
2 tbsp olive oil
2 sprigs of thyme
50g walnut halves
90g lamb's lettuce
2 smoked mackerel fillets, skin and
   any bones removed, flesh broken
   into pieces
salt and black pepper

Apple dressing
1 Granny Smith apple
3 tbsp walnut oil or olive oil
2 tbsp cider vinegar

Time check

Prep: 10 minutes
Cooking: 30 minutes

Salmon and sweet potato fishcakes

These are amazing! They are so satisfying, but the sweet potato keeps them a little lighter than usual and very tasty. I love the quinoa coating – it's nice and crunchy and so much easier to cope with than fiddling around with egg and breadcrumbs. Lovely with a tomato and watercress salad on the side.

1 Put the salmon fillets on a sheet of foil on a shallow baking tray and scatter over the spring onions, lemon zest, a squeeze of lemon juice and a tablespoon of the olive oil. Season with salt and pepper, then bake the fish for 8–10 minutes or until it's just cooked.

2 While the fish is cooking, cut the sweet potatoes into cubes. Steam or boil them for 8 minutes or until tender, then drain. (If you have a microwave, you can pierce the sweet potatoes with a fork and cook them in the microwave for 8 minutes or until tender. Leave them to cool for a few minutes, then remove the skin.)

3 Add 400g of the sweet potato to a large bowl and mash it well with a potato masher. Add the cooked salmon, spring onions, chopped herbs, chilli, if using, the beaten egg and 2 tablespoons of cooked quinoa, then season well and mix everything together. Using your hands, shape the mixture into 8 patties.

4 Tip the rest of the cooked quinoa on to a plate and spread it into an even layer. Roll each fishcake in the quinoa so it is coated all over. Place the fishcakes on a plate and pop them in the fridge for at least 20 minutes or until firm to touch. Preheat the oven to 200°C/Fan 180°C/Gas 6.

5 Lightly brush a baking tray with oil. Place the fishcakes on the baking tray and brush them with the remaining oil. Bake them for 15–20 minutes or until golden and a little crisp to touch, turning them halfway through the cooking time. Serve with lemon wedges.

Davina's tip

This is a good one to prepare in advance if that works for you. The fishcakes will be very happy in the fridge all day, ready to pop in the oven when you're home for supper.

Serves 4

453 calories per serving

3 x 140g salmon fillets, skinned and bones removed
1 bunch of spring onions, chopped
finely grated zest of ½ lemon and a squeeze of juice
2 tbsp olive oil
2 medium sweet potatoes (you need 400g cooked)
3 tbsp finely chopped chives, parsley or coriander
1 red chilli, deseeded and finely chopped (optional)
1 egg, beaten
200g ready-cooked quinoa, cold
lemon wedges, to serve
salt and black pepper

Time check

Prep: 20 minutes, plus chilling time
Cooking: 30 minutes

Grilled tuna with peppers and lentils

To make this a really easy-peasy speedy supper, I sometimes use a jar of ready-roasted peppers. You can get them in any supermarket and they do make life easier – it's surprising how many they manage to squeeze in. Otherwise you can grill and skin fresh peppers as below.

1 If you're using raw peppers, heat the grill to high, cut the peppers in half and remove the seeds. Place the peppers cut-side down on a baking tray and grill them for 10 minutes or until the skin is lightly charred. Turn them over and grill them for another 4–5 minutes. Tip the peppers into a bowl, cover them with cling film and leave them to cool for 5 minutes.

2 While the peppers are cooling, cook the tuna. Heat a griddle pan on the hob. Season the tuna steaks all over and drizzle them with a tablespoon of the oil. Place them on the smoking-hot griddle for 1–2 minutes, then turn them and cook for another 1–2 minutes on the other side for slightly rare tuna. If you prefer your tuna steaks well-cooked, leave them a little longer. Remove the steaks from the pan and keep them warm.

3 Once the peppers are cool enough to handle, remove the skin and discard it. Cut your cooked or ready-roasted peppers into thin strips, place them in a serving bowl and add the olives, capers, vinegar, herbs, lentils and the rest of the oil. Season with salt and pepper and mix everything together.

4 When you're ready to eat, scatter the rocket over the pepper mixture and serve with the tuna and some lemon wedges to squeeze over.

Davina's tip

If you prefer to cook your own lentils, you need about 100g. Rinse them well, tip them into a saucepan and cover with cold water. Bring the water to the boil and simmer for 25–30 minutes until the lentils are cooked but still have a bit of bite to them. Drain the lentils and refresh them under cold running water.

Serves 4
370 calories per serving

4 peppers (red, yellow, orange) or a jar of ready-roasted peppers
4 x 120g fresh tuna steaks
3 tbsp olive oil
100g black olives, drained
2 tbsp capers, rinsed and drained
1 tbsp red wine vinegar
2 tbsp chopped fresh basil or parsley
1 x 250g pack of ready-cooked puy lentils, rinsed
50g rocket leaves
1 lemon, cut into wedges, to serve
salt and black pepper

Time check

Prep: 15 minutes
Cooking: 20 minutes

Crunchy buttermilk chicken with roasted ratatouille

This is like a healthy version of chicken nuggets and is hugely popular with kids of all ages. Those packs of mini fillets you get in the supermarket are perfect, as you don't have to bash them flat or cut them up. Marinating the chicken in buttermilk makes it lovely and tender and you also get a deliciously creamy layer between the meat and the crumbs. Best with good crispy crumbs – see my tip below.

1 Preheat your grill to high and the oven to 200°C/Fan 180°C/Gas 6. For the ratatouille, put the courgettes, onion and aubergine pieces in a large shallow roasting tray, spreading them out into a single layer. Add the rosemary and oil and season with salt and pepper, then grill the vegetables for 10 minutes.

2 Place the chicken in a large shallow bowl and pour over the buttermilk. Cover the bowl and leave the chicken to marinate for at least 10 minutes – you can also leave it in the fridge overnight if you've planned ahead.

3 Meanwhile, in another bowl, mix together the breadcrumbs, lemon zest, rosemary and grated Parmesan and season well.

4 Remove the chicken from the buttermilk, shake off any excess and then coat each piece in the crumb mixture. Put the coated chicken on a lightly oiled baking tray, then drizzle or spray the pieces with a little oil.

5 Remove the tray of vegetables from the grill, leaving the grill on, and add the cherry tomatoes. Drizzle with balsamic, if using, transfer the tray to the hot oven and roast the vegetables for 10 minutes.

6 Grill the chicken for 15–20 minutes until golden on both sides and cooked through, turning the pieces half way through.

7 Divide the chicken between 4 plates and serve with a large green salad and lemon wedges to squeeze over.

Davina's tip

Nice crisp breadcrumbs make the best coating so if you've time, toast them in the oven first. Spread the breadcrumbs on a shallow baking tray and bake them for 5–6 minutes in the oven at 180°C/Fan 160°C/Gas 4 or until dry but not golden.

Serves 4

381 calories per serving

400g chicken mini fillets
1 x 284ml carton of buttermilk
75g wholemeal or sourdough
    breadcrumbs
finely grated zest of 1 lemon
3 sprigs of rosemary, leaves picked
    and finely chopped
25g Parmesan cheese, finely grated
2 tbsp olive oil or spray oil
1 lemon, cut into wedges, to serve
salt and black pepper

Roasted ratatouille

200g baby courgettes, cut into bite-
    size pieces
1 red onion, cut into wedges
1 aubergine, cut into bite-size pieces
1 branch of fresh rosemary
2 tbsp olive oil
4 branches of cherry tomatoes
1 tbsp balsamic vinegar (optional)

Time check

Prep: 20 minutes, plus
    marinating time
Cooking: 20 minutes

Chicken Caesar salad

A traditional Caesar salad usually contains a dressing made with raw egg, which not everyone likes, so this is an excellent egg-free version. You can prepare this a bit more quickly by grilling a chicken breast, but the beauty of my method is that the bread soaks up the juices of the chicken cooking above it, which really adds to the flavour. And you can be getting on with something else while the chicken is working its magic in the oven.

1 Preheat the oven to 200°C/Fan 180°C/Gas 6. Tear the sourdough into bite-size pieces and put them in a roasting tin. Place the chicken thighs on a rack and put the rack on the tin over the bread. Scatter the oregano and lemon zest over the chicken and season with salt and pepper, then drizzle over the olive oil. Roast for 25–30 minutes or until the chicken is golden and cooked through and the pieces of bread are crisp and golden.

2 While the chicken is cooking, make the dressing. Put the anchovy fillets into a mortar with the garlic and a little salt and bash with a pestle until the mixture forms a smooth paste. Add the yoghurt, lemon juice and grated Parmesan and season well, then add enough water to make a smooth pourable dressing – 1–2 tablespoons should do it.

3 Place the lettuce leaves in a large bowl and add the cherry tomatoes. When the chicken is cool enough to handle, strip the meat from the bones and tear it into bite-size pieces. Discard the bones.

4 Add the chicken and crispy croutons to the salad, pour over the dressing and toss together. Add a few extra shavings of Parmesan and serve at once.

Davina's tip

Some people love chicken skin while others avoid it. If you want to reduce the calories of this recipe a bit, take off the chicken skin. But if you're a big fan of crispy skin, remove the skin from the chicken after step 1 and put it on a rack under a hot grill for 3 or 4 minutes. Break the skin into pieces and add it to the salad. Yum!

Serves 4
247 calories per serving

2 slices of sourdough bread
4 chicken thighs, skin on and bone in
1 tsp dried oregano or a few fresh
    oregano leaves
finely grated zest of ½ lemon
1 tbsp olive oil
1 cos lettuce, leaves separated
    and torn
100g cherry tomatoes, halved
extra shavings of Parmesan cheese,
    to serve
salt and black pepper

Dressing
2 anchovy fillets, drained and
    chopped
1 small garlic clove, chopped
2 tbsp Greek yoghurt
2 tsp lemon juice
25g Parmesan cheese, finely grated

Time check
Prep: 20 minutes
Cooking: 30 minutes

Lamb and apricot pilaf

Lamb and rice go beautifully together and the apricots in this pilaf add a lovely sweetness. I really like the ras el hanout for a touch of Moroccan flavour – it's a mix of lots of spices so is a good time-saver and is available in supermarkets. The cooking time for the rice might vary a bit according to what kind you use, so keep an eye on it and be prepared to add a little more stock if necessary.

1 Heat the oil in a frying pan. Season the cubes of lamb and fry them for 6–8 minutes or until golden all over, turning frequently. Do this in batches if necessary so you don't overcrowd the pan. Transfer the browned lamb to a plate lined with kitchen paper and set it aside.

2 Add the onion to the pan and fry for 1–2 minutes or until softened, then add the garlic, ginger and ras el hanout and fry for another 2–3 minutes. Tip the rice into the pan and stir well to coat it in the spicy onions, then stir in the browned lamb and stock. Cover the pan with a lid and bring the stock to the boil, then turn down the heat and leave it to simmer for 15 minutes.

3 Add the chopped apricots and chickpeas and cook for another 10 minutes or until the rice has absorbed all the stock and is tender. Meanwhile, toast the almonds in a dry pan until golden.

4 Serve garnished with toasted flaked almonds and chopped mint and add a dollop of yoghurt on the side if you like.

Serves 4

609 calories per serving

1 tbsp olive oil
400g lamb neck fillet, cut into
  1cm cubes
1 large onion, finely sliced
2 garlic cloves, grated
25g fresh root ginger, grated
2 tsp ras el hanout
250g brown basmati rice
750ml hot lamb or chicken stock
75g soft dried apricots, chopped
200g canned chickpeas, drained
  and rinsed
2 tbsp flaked almonds, to garnish
2 tbsp fresh chopped mint or parsley
2 tbsp Greek yoghurt (optional)
salt and black pepper

Time check

Prep: 15 minutes
Cooking: 35 minutes

Pork fillet with mushroom sauce

This is quick to prepare but it tastes really special – an ideal supper dish if you've got friends coming round mid-week and you've been at work all day. You can do most of the preparation in advance too, which usually makes life easier. Perfect with just some steamed greens or a dish of barley couscous.

1 Preheat the oven to 180°C/Fan 160°C/Gas 4. Trim any skin off the pork fillet, then slice the pork into 12 rounds about 2cm thick. Place the pork rounds between 2 sheets of cling film and bash them with a rolling pin until they are about ½cm thick. Season the meat well with salt and pepper.

2 Heat a tablespoon of the olive oil in a large non-stick frying pan. Add the rounds of pork and fry them for 2 minutes on each side or until golden – it's best to do this in batches so you don't overcrowd the pan. Remove them from the pan and place them in a large ovenproof dish that will fit all the pork in a single layer.

3 Heat the remaining oil in the pan, add the onion and fry it over a medium heat for 5 minutes or until softened. Add the garlic and fry for another minute. Then add the mushrooms to the pan, turn up the heat and fry them for 3–4 minutes or until golden. Pour in the wine and let it bubble for 2 minutes, then add the crème fraiche and chopped sage. Simmer gently for 1–2 minutes.

4 Pour the sauce over the pork and bake for 10 minutes or until the pork is just cooked through. Serve with some barley couscous and steamed greens.

Davina's tip

You can get everything ready up to the end of step 3, then leave the pork in the fridge for up to 24 hours. Cover the dish with foil and bake at 180°C/Fan 160°C/Gas 4 for a little longer than above or until piping hot throughout – 15–20 minutes should do it.

Serves 4
484 calories per serving

600g pork fillet
2 tbsp olive oil
1 onion, thinly sliced
2 garlic cloves, finely chopped
250g chestnut mushrooms, sliced
200ml white wine
200ml crème fraiche
4 large sage leaves, chopped
salt and black pepper

Time check

Prep: 20 minutes
Cooking: 20 minutes

Squash 'spaghetti' with pancetta sauce

I'm well into spiralising now and this works brilliantly. You can use courgettes instead if you like, but you only need to cook them for 30 seconds to a minute so they don't go soggy. If you don't have a spiraliser, use a vegetable peeler or just cut the squash into long thin strands with a sharp knife.

1 Gently heat a tablespoon of the oil in a large wide shallow saucepan, add the sliced onion and season it well. Cook the onion over a medium heat for 5 minutes until softened. Add the cubes of pancetta and fry them for 2–3 minutes, then add the garlic. Finely chop half of the sage leaves, add them to the garlic and fry for another minute, then tip everything into a bowl and set aside.

2 Add the remaining whole sage leaves to the pan and fry them quickly for 20 seconds or until crisp but not coloured. Set them aside.

3 Heat the rest of the oil in the saucepan. Add the spiralised squash and a splash of water to help it steam, then cook for 2 minutes or until tender. Season well. Tip the pancetta sauce back into the pan and warm it though, while tossing the 'spaghetti' so it is evenly coated. Add a squeeze of lemon juice over the top.

4 Serve with some grated Parmesan and the crispy sage leaves scattered over the top.

Serves 4
392 calories per serving

3 tbsp olive oil
1 large white onion, finely sliced
200g cubed pancetta
2 garlic cloves, chopped
small handful of fresh sage leaves
1 large butternut squash, seeds
    removed, flesh spiralised
squeeze of lemon juice
grated Parmesan cheese, to serve
salt and black pepper

Time check

Prep: 10 minutes
Cooking: 10 minutes

Seared steak with five-bean salad

It's nice to make a little bit of meat go a long way. I do enjoy a steak once in a while and this recipe makes a good meal for four from just two steaks by serving them with a mixture of delicious beans. I'm loving edamame beans since I discovered them recently, and I find they make a great snack as well as a useful ingredient in dishes like this one.

1 Heat a griddle pan until smoking hot. Drizzle the steaks with a little oil and season them well. Sear them on the hot griddle pan for 2 minutes on each side for rare meat, then set them aside to rest for 5 minutes. Cooking times do vary according to the thickness of your steaks, but as a general guide, cook them for 3 minutes on each side for medium, and for 4 minutes on each side for well done.

2 To make the dressing, put the 40g of rocket in a small blender with the lemon zest and juice, avocado oil, mustard and half a tablespoon of water. Season well and blend until the rocket is coarsely chopped, then transfer the dressing to a jug.

3 Bring a saucepan of water to the boil, add the green beans and cook them for 2 minutes. Add the edamame beans and boil for another minute or until just tender. Drain the beans and refresh them under cold running water.

4 Mix the canned beans with the green beans, edamame and avocado in a bowl, then stir in the rocket and the cherry tomatoes, if using.

5 Cut the steaks into thick slices on the diagonal. Dish out the bean salad and add slices of steak, then top with some of the dressing. Serve the rest of the dressing alongside.

Serves 4

376 calories per serving

2 x 200g bavette or rib-eye steaks
1 tbsp olive oil
60g fine green beans, tops removed and cut in half
60g frozen edamame beans, defrosted
400g can of mixed beans, drained and rinsed
1 avocado, stone removed and flesh chopped
handful of wild rocket
handful of cherry tomatoes (optional)
salt and black pepper

Dressing

40g wild rocket
finely grated zest of ½ lemon and a squeeze of juice
3 tbsp avocado oil
1 tsp Dijon mustard

Time check

Prep: 10 minutes
Cooking: 10 minutes

—4—

Weekend specials

Tortilla lasagne 101

Spinach and ricotta filo parcels 102

Broccoli and hot-smoked salmon tart 105

Fish crumble 106

Thai sea bass with coconut rice 109

Crispy lemon thyme chicken with roasted veggies 110

Chicken, leek and mushroom pie 113

Chicken cacciatore 114

Lamb casserole with Cheddar and thyme dumplings 117

Lamb kebabs with Greek salad 118

Slow-cooked pulled pork with flatbreads and carrot, apple and beetroot slaw 120–121

Pork meatbals with pasta and tomato sauce 125

Slow-roast short rib ragu 126

Provençal beef casserole 129

Tortilla lasagne

Everyone loved the tortilla lasagne in *Smart Carbs* – it's soooo good – so we thought we would come up with another, slightly speedier version. There's lots of lovely veggies in this and it's a great recipe for a weekend lunch with all the family.

1 Preheat the oven to 200°C/Fan 180°C/Gas 6. To make the vegetable sauce, heat the oil in a saucepan and add the onion, red pepper, courgette and aubergine. Cook the vegetables over a medium heat, stirring regularly, until they have softened and the onion is translucent.

2 Add the garlic and cook for a further couple of minutes, then add the tomatoes and basil and season well. Bring the sauce to the boil and cook for 10 minutes or until the vegetables are tender. Then remove the pan from the heat and set the sauce aside to cool. Mix together the ingredients for the cheesy sauce and season with salt and pepper.

3 Assemble the lasagne in a casserole dish that's just slightly bigger than the tortilla wraps. Put a third of the vegetable sauce in the casserole dish and top with a tortilla. Spread the tortilla with a third of the cheesy mixture, then top with another tortilla. Repeat the layers, finishing with the last of the cheese sauce. If using mozzarella, tear it into pieces and arrange it on top, then sprinkle over the grated cheese, dried oregano and a little salt and black pepper.

4 Bake the lasagne in the oven for 30–35 minutes or until it is golden brown and bubbling. Leave to cool for 5 minutes in the casserole and then cut into wedges and serve with a large green salad.

Serves 6
416 calories per serving

Vegetable sauce
1 tbsp olive oil
1 large onion, finely chopped
1 large red pepper, diced
1 courgette, finely chopped
1 aubergine, finely chopped
2 garlic cloves, finely chopped
400g can of chopped tomatoes
3 tbsp fresh chopped basil
salt and black pepper

Cheesy sauce
350ml crème fraiche
50g mature Cheddar cheese, grated
grating of nutmeg
1 tbsp grated Parmesan cheese

To assemble
6 corn tortilla wraps
1 ball of mozzarella (optional)
30g mature Cheddar cheese, grated
1 tsp dried oregano

Time check

Prep: 20 minutes
Cooking: 45 minutes

Spinach and ricotta filo parcels

You can serve these hot or cold but I think they are totally amazing straight out of the oven. They do keep well for a couple of days in an airtight container – if they last that long – and you can warm them up in the oven for 10 minutes before serving. For a change, you could use crumbled feta cheese instead of ricotta.

1 Preheat the oven to 200°C/Fan 180°C/Gas 6. Heat the oil in a large frying pan, add the onion and fry it for 2–3 minutes or until softened. Add the garlic and pine nuts and fry for another 2 minutes.

2 Add the spinach and cook it for 3 minutes or until wilted. Tip everything into a bowl, draining off any excess water. Add the lemon zest, a squeeze of juice and the ricotta and season with salt and pepper. Set aside to cool.

3 Place a sheet of filo on a large board, brush it with melted butter, then repeat with 2 more sheets of filo until you have 3 layers of pastry. Cut the filo into 4 strips along the length of the pastry.

4 Place a tablespoonful of the spinach mix on the end of a strip, leaving a 2cm border. Take the right-hand corner and fold it diagonally to the left, enclosing the filling and forming a triangle. Fold again along the upper crease of the triangle. Keep folding in this way until you reach the end of the strip. Brush the outer surface with more butter. Place the parcel on a baking tray and cover it with a clean tea towel while you make 3 more parcels.

5 Repeat steps 3 and 4 with the remaining sheets of filo and the rest of the spinach mixture to make another 8 parcels. Bake them in the centre of the oven for 12–15 minutes or until golden and crisp, then serve while they're still warm.

Makes 12 parcels

199 calories per parcel

1 tbsp olive oil
1 red onion, finely sliced
2 garlic cloves, finely chopped
30g pine nuts
300g spinach
finely grated zest of 1 lemon and a squeeze of juice
150g ricotta, drained
9 sheets of filo pastry
90g melted butter
salt and black pepper

Time check

Prep: 25 minutes
Cooking: 20–25 minutes

Broccoli and hot-smoked salmon tart

Now this recipe does take a little more time, but it's something I love to cook at the weekend. I don't often make my own pastry but when I do I love this nutty version. And if I can manage it so can you! I'm a big fan of hot-smoked salmon – it's so delicious and very easy to use. Serve this with a big green salad and everyone will be happy.

1 Put the walnuts in a food processor and blitz them until finely ground. Add the flour, butter and a large pinch of salt, then pulse until the mixture just comes together into a ball. Add a little more flour if it still seems sticky. Wrap the pastry in cling film and leave it to chill in the fridge for 30 minutes.

2 Cook the broccoli in boiling water for 3 minutes, then plunge it into a bowl of iced water to cool and stop the cooking process. Drain the broccoli, pat it dry with kitchen paper and set it aside.

3 Roll the pastry out on a lightly floured surface until it's the thickness of a pound coin. Line a 20cm fluted, loose-bottomed flan tin with the pastry and pop it into the freezer to chill for 10 minutes. You might have a bit of pastry left over depending on how thinly you've managed to roll it.

4 Preheat the oven to 200°C/Fan 180°C/Gas 6. Prick the pastry base all over with a fork, cover it with greaseproof paper and fill it with baking beans. Bake the pastry for 15 minutes or until it is just set, then remove the beans and paper and put the pastry back in the oven for 5 minutes or until it's light golden and crisp. Turn the oven down to 150°C/Fan 130°C/Gas 2.

5 Put the crème fraiche in a bowl and add the eggs, mustard and half the chives, then season with salt and pepper. Flake the salmon into pieces and arrange it in the pastry case with the broccoli. Pour over the cream mixture, then sprinkle with grated Parmesan and the reserved chives. Bake the tart for 30–35 minutes or until the filling is set and serve hot or at room temperature.

Serves 8
419 calories per serving

75g walnut halves
150g wholemeal spelt flour
100g cold butter, cubed
150g tenderstem broccoli, trimmed weight
400ml crème fraiche
2 large eggs
½ tsp English mustard
2 tbsp chives, finely chopped
125g hot-smoked salmon, skin and bones removed
2–3 tbsp finely grated Parmesan cheese
salt and black pepper

Time check

Prep: 30 minutes, plus chilling time
Cooking: 50 minutes

Fish crumble

The chicken crumble in *Smart Carbs* was a winner so we've come up with a fabulous fishy version. It's a fish pie revolution. I like using broccoli in the topping, but you can go with cauliflower if you prefer. Nice with some green veggies, such as buttered peas.

1 Preheat the oven to 200°C/Fan 180°C/Gas 6. Heat the butter in a large saucepan. Add the leeks, season them with salt and pepper, then fry them over a low heat until softened. Add the flour and stir to coat the slices of leek.

2 Slowly add the milk, whisking continuously until it is combined, then add the crème fraiche and dill. The sauce will be thick at this point, but the fish will loosen it slightly as it cooks. Take the pan off the heat and stir in the prawns and fish, then tip the mixture into an ovenproof dish.

3 For the topping, break the broccoli into pieces, put them in a food processor and blitz until the mixture resembles breadcrumbs. Heat the olive oil in a large frying pan. Add the broccoli and the quinoa and fry for at least 5 minutes until they start to turn a light golden brown. Remove the pan from the heat and check the seasoning.

4 Spoon the topping over the fish filling, then sprinkle over the Parmesan and dot with butter. Put the crumble in the oven and bake it for 20 minutes until the topping has browned round the edges and the filling is piping hot.

Davina's tip

If you want to cook your own quinoa, use 75g of raw quinoa and cook according to the packet instructions.

Serves 6

354 calories per serving

25g butter
3 leeks, thinly sliced
3 tbsp wholemeal spelt flour
400ml whole milk
3 tbsp crème fraiche
2 tbsp chopped dill
150g raw shelled king prawns
400g mix of skinless raw salmon, cod
    and undyed smoked haddock, cut
    into large cubes
salt and black pepper

Topping
150g broccoli
2 tbsp olive oil
150g ready-cooked quinoa
15g Parmesan cheese, grated
10g butter

Time check

Prep: 20 minutes
Cooking: 30 minutes

Thai sea bass with coconut rice

I love Thai flavours and this is such a fabulously easy way of cooking fish. You can get the parcel of sea bass ready in advance and keep it in the fridge, then pop it in the oven at the last minute. Coconut rice is a perfect partner for the fish but you could serve it with plain brown rice if you're short of time.

1 First prepare the coconut rice. Heat the olive oil in a large saucepan, add the onion and fry it over a gentle heat for about 10 minutes or until softened but not coloured. Add the ginger and fry for 2–3 minutes. Add the rinsed, drained rice and stir well to coat the grains of rice in the oil. Pour in the wine, turn up the heat to high and let it bubble for 1–2 minutes to burn off the alcohol.

2 Add the lemongrass, stock and coconut milk to the pan. Bring to the boil, then cover the pan with a lid, turn down the heat and leave to simmer for 20–25 minutes or until tender. The exact timing will depend on the brand of rice you use. Top up with more stock or water if it starts to look dry.

3 Remove the pan from the heat and discard the lemongrass. The rice should have absorbed all the stock and be nice and tender. Stir in the chopped coriander just before serving.

4 While the rice is cooking, prepare the sea bass. Preheat the oven to 200°C/Fan 180°C/Gas 6. Cut a piece of foil large enough to wrap the sea bass fillets up loosely. Brush the foil with oil, then place 2 of the fillets side by side, skin-side down, on the foil. Scatter the lemongrass, lime leaves, lime zest and juice, chilli and coriander over the fillets and season with salt and pepper. Place the other 2 fillets on top to make 2 fish sandwiches. Scrunch together the foil so it is sealed but allow a little space around the fish. Bake for 12 minutes or until the fish is just cooked – thicker fillets will take longer.

5 Remove the sea bass from the oven, separate the fillets and serve them with the rice and lime wedges to squeeze over.

Serves 4
696 calories per serving

4 sea bass fillets
oil, for brushing
1 lemongrass stick, sliced
4 Kaffir lime leaves,
zest and juice of 2 limes
1 red chilli, deseeded and sliced
handful of fresh coriander, chopped
1 lime, cut into wedges, to serve
salt and black pepper

Coconut rice
1 tbsp olive oil
1 large onion, finely sliced
15g fresh root ginger, finely chopped
300g brown basmati rice
150ml white wine
1 lemongrass stick, bashed
400ml fresh chicken or vegetable
   stock
200ml coconut milk
handful of fresh coriander, chopped

Time check

Prep: 20 minutes
Cooking: 35 minutes

Crispy lemon thyme chicken with roasted veggies

Mmmm, a one-pot dish – I do love a one-pot and this is a great one to make at the weekend. It's quick to prepare and although it does take a while to cook, you can go off and play with the kids or do your fitness routine while supper is looking after itself in the oven. Make sure you cut the vegetables into cubes roughly the same size so that they cook evenly. If you want to reduce the calories in this dish, remove the chicken skin before serving.

1 Preheat the oven to 200°C/Fan 180°C/Gas 6. Place the sweet potato, celeriac, carrot and garlic in a large shallow roasting tin. Drizzle them with a tablespoon of the oil and season with salt and pepper, then roast for 15 minutes.

2 Add the beetroot to the roasting tin and nestle the chicken thighs in among the vegetables. Drizzle with the rest of the oil and scatter over the lemon zest, a squeeze of lemon juice and the thyme and season well. Place the other (unsqueezed) lemon half in the tin, cut-side up. Roast on the top shelf of the oven for 30 minutes.

3 Turn the oven up to 220°C/Fan 200°C/Gas 7. Sprinkle the vinegar over the vegetables and roast for another 5–10 minutes. The vegetables should be beautifully tender and the chicken cooked through with lovely crispy skin. Scatter with rocket leaves before serving.

Davina's tip

You can get ahead with this one if you like – prepare everything up to the end of step 2, then cool, cover with cling film and chill in the fridge for 24 hours. You may need to increase the cooking time for step 3 by 5 minutes if the dish is straight from the fridge.

Serves 4

352 calories per serving

1 medium sweet potato, cut into cubes (about 250g peeled weight)
½ celeriac, cut into cubes (about 200g peeled weight)
1 large carrot, cut into chunks
4 garlic cloves, unpeeled
2 tbsp olive oil
300g pack of cooked beetroot, cut into wedges
8 chicken thighs, skin on
finely grated zest of l lemon and a squeeze of juice
2 sprigs of lemon or normal thyme, leaves picked
1 tbsp cider vinegar
30g rocket leaves
salt and black pepper

Time check

Prep: 15 minutes
Cooking: 50–55 minutes

Chicken, leek and mushroom pie

Who doesn't love a pie (?!) and this crunchy filo topping is a little lighter than the usual pastry. If you want to get ahead, you can prepare this up to the end of step 4, then cover it with cling film and leave it in the fridge for up to 2 days. You'll need to cook the pie for a little longer to make sure the sauce is bubbling hot throughout.

1 Preheat the oven to 200°C/Fan 180°C/Gas 6. Heat a tablespoon of the oil in a large saucepan and add the mushrooms. Season them with salt and pepper and fry for 3 minutes over a high heat or until golden. Remove the mushrooms from the pan and set them aside.

2 Heat the rest of the oil in the pan. Add the leeks and fry them for 5 minutes or until softened, adding 1–2 tablespoons of water to help them steam. Once the water has evaporated, add the chicken to the pan, season with salt and pepper and fry for another 5 minutes. Sprinkle in the flour and stir well to coat the leeks and chicken.

3 Gradually add the chicken stock, crème fraiche, thyme leaves and the mustard, if using. Bring everything to the boil and then simmer for 5 minutes until thickened. Spoon the mixture into a large 20 x 30cm ovenproof dish.

4 Place the sheets of filo in a pile and cut them into 4 strips across the longest length – you'll end up with 24 strips of the same size. Brush each strip with melted butter, scrunch it up into a loose ball, then place it on top of the filling – it should be almost covered with filo balls.

5 Put the pie in the centre of the oven and bake it for 20–25 minutes or until the sauce is bubbling hot and the filo is crisp and golden. Serve it up at once.

Serves 4

569 calories per serving

2 tbsp olive oil
200g button or chestnut mushrooms, quartered
2 medium leeks, thickly sliced
400g boneless chicken thighs, cut into bite-size pieces
3 tbsp spelt flour
450ml hot chicken stock
100ml crème fraiche
3 sprigs of fresh thyme, leaves picked
1 tsp grainy mustard (optional)
6 sheets filo pastry
30g butter, melted

Time check

Prep: 20 minutes
Cooking: 40 minutes

Chicken cacciatore

Chicken thighs are cheap and tasty and they're perfect for my easy version of an Italian classic. This is such a comforting dish and I do love a bubbling bake. It's just right served with barley couscous and some greens such as beans or broccoli.

1 Preheat the oven to 200°C/Fan 180°C/Gas 6. Heat a tablespoon of the oil in a large frying pan over a medium heat. Add the onions and peppers and fry them for 3–4 minutes or until slightly softened. Add the garlic and fry for another minute. Tip the peppers and garlic into a large ovenproof dish and set aside.

2 Drizzle the chicken pieces with the rest of the oil, season them well, then add them to the pan and fry until golden brown all over – you might need to do this in batches. Place the browned chicken on top of the onions and peppers in the oven dish.

3 Pour the cherry tomatoes into the frying pan, add the chilli flakes, if using, and season, then warm the tomatoes through for a minute over a low heat. Tip the tomatoes into the dish with the chicken and vegetables, then add the rosemary sprigs or oregano. Cover the dish with foil and bake in the oven for 30 minutes.

4 After 30 minutes, remove the foil, scatter the olives into the dish and bake for another 15 minutes, uncovered, or until the chicken is cooked through.

Serves 4
373 calories per serving

2 tbsp olive oil
2 red onions, cut into wedges
3 peppers, red, orange and yellow,
    deseeded and cut into strips
2 garlic cloves, chopped
8 chicken thighs, skin on and bone in
2 x 400g cans of cherry tomatoes
pinch of chilli flakes (optional)
2 sprigs of rosemary or 2 tsp dried
    oregano
50g pitted Kalamata olives
salt and black pepper

Time check

Prep: 20 minutes
Cooking: 45 minutes

Lamb casserole with Cheddar and thyme dumplings

Warming and cosy, this is just the dish to cheer up a winter weekend. It's low on effort and high on taste, and it's lovely to see – and smell – this simmering away on the hob. Some green veg is all you need on the side.

1 Heat the oil in a large flameproof casserole dish over a high heat. Season the cubes of lamb with salt and pepper, add them to the casserole dish and fry until golden all over – best to do this in batches so you don't overcrowd the dish. Remove the lamb as it is browned and set it aside on a plate lined with kitchen paper.

2 Add the celery, leek and carrots to the dish and fry them for 3–4 minutes. Sprinkle in the flour and stir well to coat all the vegetables.

3 Put the lamb back in the dish, pour in the wine and let it bubble for a few minutes to burn off the alcohol. Add the stock and the bouquet garni, then bring everything to the boil. Put a lid on the dish and leave to simmer for 40 minutes until the lamb is tender.

4 At the end of the 40 minutes, remove the lid and check the sauce. It should have reduced and be slightly thickened, but if not just cook for a few minutes more, uncovered, until you have the desired consistency. Remove the bouquet garni.

5 While the stew is cooking, make the dumplings. Mix the flour and baking powder in a large bowl. Add the cubes of cold butter and rub them into the flour with your fingertips until the mixture resembles breadcrumbs. Add the mustard, if using, the cheese and thyme leaves and season, then mix in a splash of water (1–2 tablespoons) to make a soft dough.

6 Divide the dough into 8 pieces and roll them into balls. Place the dumplings on top of the stew, put the lid on and simmer over a low heat for 10–15 minutes or until the dumplings are cooked through and beautifully puffed up. Serve with some green vegetables.

Davina's tip

If you want to make your own bouquet garni, take 2 bay leaves and a few sprigs of fresh thyme, rosemary and parsley and tie them together with string.

Serves 4
571 calories per serving

1 tbsp olive oil
500g lamb neck fillet, cut into
    3cm cubes
2 celery sticks, thickly sliced
1 leek, thickly sliced
2 carrots, thickly sliced
2 tbsp wholemeal spelt flour
150ml white wine
800ml hot lamb or chicken stock
1 bouquet garni
salt and black pepper

Cheddar and thyme dumplings
125g spelt flour
1 tsp baking powder
50g cold butter, cut into cubes
2 tsp grainy mustard (optional)
30g mature Cheddar cheese, grated
2 sprigs of thyme, leaves picked

Time check

Prep: 25 minutes
Cooking: 1 hour

Lamb kebabs with Greek salad

Even just half an hour marinating does something magical to meat, making it extra tender and delicious, and these lamb kebabs with a lovely Greek salad are a huge favourite of mine. There's bags of flavour here for very little work – just the thing when you're in a hurry for a good meal.

1 Cut the lamb into cubes and the onion and peppers into bite-size pieces. Cut the courgette into thick slices. Put them and all the other kebab ingredients into a large bowl and season well, then cover and leave to marinate for at least 30 minutes – or overnight in the fridge if time allows.

2 Thread pieces of meat and vegetables alternately on to 4 large or 8 small metal skewers. Preheat the grill to high. Place the skewers on a large roasting tray and grill them for 15–20 minutes or until they're lightly charred and the meat is cooked. Turn the skewers frequently.

3 While the skewers are cooking, prepare the salad. Quarter the vine tomatoes and cut the cherry tomatoes in half. Cut the cucumber and feta into cubes. Put all the salad ingredients in a large bowl, season and toss together.

4 Serve the hot skewers with the Greek salad.

Davina's tip

A bowl of tzatziki adds the perfect finishing touch here. You can buy good tzatziki in the supermarket or it's very easy to make your own.

Take half a cucumber, remove the seeds with a teaspoon and then grate the cucumber into a clean tea towel. Squeeze to remove the excess liquid, then tip the cucumber into a bowl. Add 200g Greek yoghurt, half a teaspoon of cumin, a tablespoon of chopped mint and a crushed garlic clove, then mix well. Finish with a squeeze of lemon and season with salt and pepper.

Serves 4
490 calories per serving

500g lamb neck fillet
1 red onion
1 red, 1 yellow and 1 orange pepper, deseeded
1 courgette
1 tsp ground cumin
2 tsp ras el hanout
2 garlic cloves, finely chopped
2 tbsp chopped fresh oregano
finely grated zest of 1 lemon and a squeeze of juice
salt and black pepper

Greek salad
200g vine tomatoes
100g cherry tomatoes
1 cucumber
100g feta cheese
½ red onion, thinly sliced
100g pitted Kalamata olives
1 tbsp red wine vinegar
3 tbsp extra virgin olive oil
2 tbsp chopped fresh oregano

Time check

Prep: 15 minutes, plus marinating time
Cooking: 20 minutes

Slow-cooked pulled pork

This is definitely one for a family Sunday treat. Yes, it has a long cooking time but it can look after itself so once it's in the oven you can forget about it and just enjoy the tantalising cooking smells. And it's perfect with the flatbreads and slaw as a change from regular Sunday roast dishes. BTW, if you have a double oven you can start cooking the crackling 20 minutes before the pork has finished cooking.

1 Preheat the oven to 220°C/Fan 200°C/Gas 7. Score the pork skin and then carefully remove the skin from the meat with a sharp knife, leaving a small layer of fat – or make life easy for yourself and ask your butcher to do this for you! Pour boiling water over the skin and then pat it dry with kitchen paper. Leave it in the fridge uncovered until the pork is almost ready. This drying and chilling will help crisp the skin.

2 Line a large roasting tin with a sheet of foil big enough to fold over the top of the pork. Mix together the mustard powder, garlic powder, cinnamon, paprika and thyme in a small bowl and season with salt and pepper. Pat the pork dry with kitchen paper, then spread the mixture all over the meat. Drizzle with the oil.

3 Place the pork on the foil in the tin and put it in the hot oven, uncovered, for 20 minutes or until the meat is golden brown on top. Take the meat out and turn the oven down to 150°C/Fan 130°C/Gas 2. Pour the maple syrup over the pork, scatter the onions around it, then add 100ml of water. Wrap the foil around the meat to make a sealed parcel. Put the tin back in the oven and cook the pork for about 4 hours until it is soft enough to break apart with 2 forks.

4 Remove the pork from the oven, unwrap it, then carefully pour off the juices and set them aside.

5 Turn the oven up to 220°C/Fan 200°C/Gas 7. Put the pork skin on a baking tray, scatter it with sea salt, then rub it all in so it goes into the scores. Roast the skin for 15–20 minutes or until it's puffed up, crisp and golden. Break it into pieces and set aside.

6 Skim the excess fat from the reserved cooking juices and warm them through in a small pan. Pour a little over the pork and serve the rest in a warm jug to add at the table.

Serves 6
349 calories per serving (pork)

1.6kg pork shoulder, bone in
2 tsp English mustard powder
½ tsp garlic powder
½ tsp ground cinnamon
2 tsp smoked paprika
small handful of thyme sprigs
1 tbsp olive oil
2 tbsp maple syrup
2 onions, cut into wedges
sea salt and black pepper

Time check
Prep: 10 minutes
Cooking: 4 hours 40 minutes

Flatbreads

1 Melt the butter in a small pan and then mix it with the milk in a jug.

2 Put the flours, your choice of flavouring (seeds or herbs), a teaspoon of salt and a good grinding of black pepper into a bowl. Make a well in the middle and then gradually pour in the butter and milk mixture. Stir with a wooden spoon until the mixture comes together into a ball.

3 Tip the dough out on to a lightly floured surface and knead it for a good 2 minutes. Wrap the dough in cling film and leave it to rest for 30 minutes.

4 Cut the dough into 8 pieces and roll them into balls. Then, using a rolling pin, roll out each ball as thinly as possible on a lightly floured board.

5 Pour a dash of oil into a large frying pan and place the pan over a medium heat. Put a flatbread into the pan, cook it for 1–2 minutes or until it is beginning to bubble up and then flip it over with a spatula and fry for another minute on the other side.

6 Transfer the flatbread to a plate lined with a clean tea towel and cover it with the tea towel to keep it warm. Repeat until you've cooked all the flatbreads, then serve them warm.

Makes 8

238 calories per flatbread

50g butter
175ml whole milk
150g chickpea flour
150g wholemeal spelt flour, plus extra
    for rolling
2 tsp cumin or onion seeds or 2 tbsp
    chopped fresh coriander
3 tbsp olive oil
salt and black pepper

Time check

Prep: 10 minutes,
    plus resting time
Cooking: 10 minutes

Carrot, apple and beetroot slaw

1 Start by mixing the dressing ingredients in a large bowl. Season with salt and pepper and mix well.

2 Add the grated celeriac, apple, beetroot and carrots and toss everything well to coat in the dressing ingredients.

3 Cover and chill in the fridge until needed. Sprinkle with sesame seed, then serve.

Time check

Prep: 15 minutes
Cooking: 0 minutes

Serves 6

230 calories per serving

200g celeriac, coarsely grated
1 Granny Smith apple, coarsely grated
1 large raw beetroot, coarsely grated
2 carrots, coarsely grated
2 tbsp white and black sesame seeds

Dressing
100g Greek yoghurt
2 tbsp grainy mustard
finely grated zest of ½ orange and
    2 tbsp orange juice
2 tbsp extra virgin olive oil
1 tbsp sesame oil
3 tbsp chopped fresh basil
salt and black pepper

Pork meatballs with pasta and tomato sauce

This is a seriously useful supper dish. It's great served with pasta, as here, or you can have just the meatballs and sauce with salad or some spiralised veg if you're avoiding carbs. Whichever way – it's delicious. Here's a little tip I've learned: if the tomato sauce tastes a bit sharp, just add a teaspoon of honey.

1 For the sauce, heat the oil in a large saucepan. Add the onion, season well and fry it over a gentle heat until softened but not coloured. Add the garlic and oregano and fry for 1–2 minutes. Now pour in the wine, turn up the heat and let it bubble for 3–4 minutes, then add the rest of the sauce ingredients. Bring everything to the boil, then turn down the heat, put a lid on the pan and simmer the sauce for 20 minutes or until thickened slightly. Add a splash of water if the sauce gets too thick.

2 While the sauce is bubbling, make the meatballs. Heat the oil in a frying pan, add the leek and sage and fry until the leek is softened but not coloured. Remove the pan from the heat and leave to cool.

3 Preheat your grill to medium hot. Tip the cooled leeks into a large bowl, add the sausage meat, lemon zest and egg. Season with salt and pepper and mix until well combined. Using wet hands, shape the mixture into 16 bite-size balls.

4 Place the meatballs on a lightly oiled baking tray and grill them for 15 minutes until golden brown and cooked through, turning frequently.

5 Meanwhile, cook the pasta according to the packet instructions. Tip the meatballs into the tomato sauce and heat through. Serve with the pasta and some grated Parmesan if you like.

Davina's tip

As this dish freezes well you could make double quantities so you have some for another time. Leave the meatballs and tomato sauce to cool completely, then tip everything into a freezer-proof container and freeze for up to 1 month. Defrost overnight in the fridge, then reheat in a saucepan over a very gentle heat until piping hot throughout.

Serves 4

496 calories per serving

2 tbsp olive oil
1 leek, finely chopped
4 fresh sage leaves, finely chopped
350g good-quality pork sausages, skinned
finely grated zest of ½ lemon
1 egg, beaten
200g wholemeal spaghetti or penne
freshly grated Parmesan cheese, to serve (optional)
salt and black pepper

Tomato sauce

1 tbsp olive oil
1 medium onion, finely chopped
2 garlic cloves, finely chopped
1 tsp dried oregano
75ml white wine
2 x 400g cans of chopped tomatoes
pinch of dried chilli flakes (optional)
small handful of basil leaves, chopped

Time check

Prep: 20 minutes
Cooking: 30 minutes

Slow-roast short rib ragu

This is definitely one to make at the weekend when you're at home and it doesn't matter that it has to bubble away in the oven for several hours – the longer the better. The prep is super quick though and can be done in a hurry, so you can have a real feast with very little effort. This recipe makes enough sauce to serve eight with pasta, but you can always pop half in the freezer to enjoy another time.

1 Preheat the oven to 180°C/Fan 160°C/Gas 4. Heat a tablespoon of the oil in a frying pan, season the short ribs and fry them for 3–4 minutes or until golden on all sides.

2 Put the browned ribs in a large roasting tin and add the onion, carrots and celery. Drizzle them with the remaining oil, then roast them in the oven for 45 minutes. Add the garlic, tomatoes, wine, bouquet garni and stock and roast for another 2 hours or longer – until the beef is really tender. It should be falling off the bone so you can shred the meat with 2 forks.

3 When the meat has reached this stage, take the roasting tin out of the oven and set it aside until the ribs are cool enough to handle. Pull the meat off the bones, then discard the bones and the bouquet garni. Tip everything else into a saucepan and mash gently so that all the flavours merge together. Have a taste and season with salt and pepper as needed.

4 Cook the pasta according to the packet instructions, then serve with the sauce and garnish with basil. Serve with a bowl of grated Parmesan to add at the table.

Serves 8

491 calories per serving (with pasta)

2 tbsp olive oil
1kg beef short ribs
1 large red onion, chopped
2 carrots, chopped
2 celery sticks, chopped
4 garlic cloves, unpeeled
2 x 400g cans of plum or cherry tomatoes
200ml red wine
1 bouquet garni made up of bay, thyme and rosemary
500ml hot beef stock
600g wholewheat spaghetti or penne
basil leaves, to garnish
grated Parmesan cheese, to serve
salt and black pepper

Time check

Prep: 15 minutes
Cooking: 3 hours or more

Provençal beef casserole

This is a great family meal but also perfect for a weekend supper with friends. It's another dish that you can put together quickly, then forget about – I love them!

1 Preheat the oven to 160°C/Fan 140C/Gas 3. Heat the oil in a flameproof casserole dish, season the cubes of beef and fry them for 4–5 minutes or until browned all over, turning the cubes frequently. It's probably best to do this in batches so you don't overcrowd the pan. Transfer each batch to a plate lined with kitchen paper as it is browned.

2 Add the bacon and onion and fry for 5 minutes or until softened, then add the garlic and fry for 1 minute. Sprinkle in the flour and fry for another minute.

3 Tip the browned beef back into the pan, pour in the wine and let it bubble for 4 minutes or until it has reduced by half. Add the stock, chopped tomatoes, bouquet garni and strips of orange peel, then bring to the boil. Cover the dish with a lid and put it in the oven for 2 hours or until the meat is really tender.

4 Remove the dish from the oven and add the baby carrots, then put it back in the oven for another 20 minutes or until the carrots are tender. Take the dish out of the oven again and remove the orange peel and the bouquet garni, then stir in the olives. Scatter with chopped parsley and orange zest and serve with barley couscous and greens.

Davina's tip

This freezes amazingly well. Cook it to the end of step 3 – don't add the carrots or olives. Let it cool completely, then tip it into a freezer-proof container and freeze for up to 1 month. Defrost fully, remove the orange peel and bouquet garni, then add the carrots and olives. Heat until piping hot before serving with the garnishes as above.

Serves 6
482 calories per serving

2 tbsp olive oil
1kg beef shin or braising steak, cut into 3cm cubes
150g smoked bacon, cut into thin strips
1 onion, halved and thinly sliced
2 garlic cloves, thinly sliced
2 tbsp spelt flour
600ml red wine, such as Cabernet Sauvignon
200ml hot beef stock
400g can of chopped tomatoes
1 bouquet garni (see p.117)
2 strips of thinly pared orange peel
150g baby carrots, tops removed
75g black olives
3 tbsp finely chopped parsley leaves, to serve
finely grated zest of 1 orange, to serve
salt and black pepper

Time check

Prep: 25 minutes
Cooking: 3 hours

—5—
Guilt-free snacks

Healthy nachos with tomato salsa 133
Crispy cauli cheese bites 134
Spicy squash hummus 137
Carrot and seed crackers 138
White bean and rosemary dip with tortilla crisps 141
Sesame kale crisps 142
Seedy soda bread 145
Nut butters 146
Giant crispbreads 149
Warm anchovy dip 150
Apple and cheese scones 153
Prune and almond chocolate truffles 154
Chocolate, cherry and almond fudge 157
Fruit and nut cookies 158
Smoothies 160–161

Healthy nachos with tomato salsa

My family are just crazy for nachos so we like to make our own – that way we know exactly what we're eating. You could also serve these with guacamole and there's a recipe in my *5 Weeks to Sugar-Free* book. The salsa is totally uh-mazing. I sometimes just like to eat it with a spoon.

1 Preheat the oven to 180°C/Fan 160°C/Gas 4. Cut the tortillas into triangles and place them on a baking tray. Brush or spray them with a little oil and season with salt and paprika, then bake for 6–8 minutes or until they're just golden and crisp, turning once. Sprinkle the hot chips with finely grated lime zest and set aside.

2 Prepare the tomato salsa. Place all the salsa ingredients in a serving bowl, add a little salt and pepper, then mix together.

3 Preheat the grill to high. Scatter the grated cheese over the tortilla chips and grill them for 1–2 minutes or until the cheese is just melted but not scorched. Serve the hot chips with the tomato salsa to dip into.

Serves 4

299 calories per serving
399 calories per serving
(with salsa)

4 corn tortillas
1–2 tbsp olive oil or light spray oil
½ tsp smoked paprika
finely grated zest of 1 lime,
150g mature Cheddar cheese,
    coarsely grated
sea salt

Tomato salsa

300g cherry tomatoes, cut into
    quarters
¼ red onion, finely chopped
½ long red chilli, deseeded and finely
    chopped
1 tbsp red wine vinegar
3 tbsp extra virgin olive oil
2 tbsp chopped fresh basil leaves
salt and black pepper

Time check

Prep: 10 minutes
Cooking: 10 minutes

Crispy cauli cheese bites

All the family love these crispy little goodies – a sort of riff on our favourite cauliflower cheese. Serve them straight from the oven and they disappear in seconds. The great thing is that you can get them ready up to 24 hours ahead, keep them in the fridge, then cook them when you're ready. BTW, don't skip crisping up the breadcrumbs – it really does make a difference.

1 Put the cauliflower florets in a steamer over a pan of boiling water and steam them for 2 minutes. If you don't have a steamer, put the florets in a colander that fits snugly inside a pan, cover with a lid and steam as before. Don't cook the florets for any longer than 2 minutes, though, or they will go soggy! Set them aside to cool while you prepare the breadcrumbs.

2 Preheat the oven to 180°C/Fan 160°C/Gas 4. Put the bread in a food processor and blitz it to crumbs. Spread the crumbs out on a baking tray and put them in the oven for 10 minutes or until crisp.

3 Turn the oven up to 220°C/Fan 200°C/Gas 7. Pour the buttermilk into a shallow bowl. Mix the crumbs, Parmesan and rosemary in another shallow bowl and season with salt and pepper.

4 Dip a cauliflower floret in buttermilk and shake off any excess. Then dip it into the crumb mix and place it on a non-stick baking tray. Repeat to coat all the cauliflower florets. Spray them lightly with spray oil, then bake for 20–25 minutes or until they're lovely and golden and crisp all over.

5 For the dip, mix all the ingredients together in a bowl and season with salt and pepper.

6 When the cauliflower bites are ready, tip them into a serving dish and serve at once with the cheesy dip.

Serves 4
256 calories per serving

1 small cauliflower, cut into bite-size florets
75g sourdough or wholemeal bread
200ml buttermilk
3 tbsp finely grated Parmesan cheese
3 sprigs of rosemary, finely chopped
spray oil
salt and black pepper

Cheesy dip
150ml soured cream
2 tbsp finely chopped chives
20g mature Cheddar cheese, grated

Time check

Prep: 20 minutes
Cooking: 35 minutes

Spicy squash hummus

Everyone likes the trad hummus but it's good to vary it sometimes. In this version, squash and spices add sweetness and flavour to a classic mix.

1 Preheat the oven to 200°C/Fan 180°C/Gas 6. Put the butternut squash and unpeeled garlic into a shallow roasting tray and coat them with the oil. Sprinkle over the chilli flakes and spices and season well with salt and pepper. Pour in 100ml of water, then cover the tray with foil and roast the squash for 30 minutes or until tender. At the end of the cooking time, remove the foil and leave the squash to cool slightly.

2 Tip the cooled squash into a food processor with all the roasting juices from the tin. Squeeze the garlic out of the skins into the food processor and discard the skins. Add the chickpeas, tahini and a squeeze of lemon juice, then blitz until you have the consistency you like.

3 Spoon the hummus into a serving bowl. Add a swirl of olive oil and a scattering of dried chilli flakes, if using, then serve with crispbreads (see p.149), corn tortilla crisps (see p.141), or sticks of raw vegetables.

Serves 4 generously
204 calories per serving

400g butternut squash, cut into cubes
3 garlic cloves, unpeeled
2 tbsp olive oil, plus extra to serve
pinch of chilli flakes, plus extra to
    garnish
1 tsp ground cumin
1 tsp ground coriander
400g can of chickpeas, drained
    and rinsed
2 tbsp tahini
squeeze of lemon juice
pinch of dried chilli flakes (optional)
salt and black pepper

Time check

Prep: 15 minutes
Cooking: 30 minutes

Carrot and seed crackers

Good crackers are hard to find so I've started making my own. That way I know exactly what's in them too. These are quite crumbly but if you spread the mixture nice and thinly they will hold together fine. Store them in a sealed container and they keep well for three or four days.

1 Preheat the oven to 200°C/Fan 180°C/Gas 6.

2 Toast the almonds in a dry frying pan for a few minutes, then set them aside to cool. Put the almonds into a food processor and pulse a few times until they are coarsely chopped. Add the seeds (reserving the half tablespoon of cumin seeds for later) and pulse a few more times until everything is combined but still coarsely chopped.

3 Add the carrots, sun-dried tomato paste, olive oil and a tablespoon of cold water, then season with a teaspoon of sea salt and some black pepper. Blend until the mixture is sticky and holds together if you pinch a bit in your fingers, but is still quite coarsely chopped.

4 Lightly oil a baking tray and spread the mixture over it to a thickness of about ½cm. Smooth it flat with wet hands and sprinkle with the remaining cumin seeds.

5 Bake the crackers in the oven for 15–20 minutes or until they are lightly golden and firm to touch. Remove them from the oven, trim the edges and discard, then cut into 25 rectangles. Carefully turn them over and put them back in the oven for another 6–8 minutes to crisp them up a little more. Take them out and leave to cool on the baking tray for 5 minutes, and then transfer them to a cooling rack to cool.

Davina's tip

To serve, spread with light cream cheese, sliced tomatoes and a few basil leaves or sliced avocado, a squeeze of lime and a sprinkling of toasted sesame seeds. You can also use these crackers instead of crisps for scooping up dips.

Makes 25 crackers
80 calories per cracker

100g blanched almonds, lightly toasted
50g sunflower seeds
50g pumpkin seeds
50g sesame seeds
2 tbsp golden linseeds
1½ tbsp cumin seeds
2 large carrots, coarsely grated (about 200g)
4 tbsp sun-dried tomato paste
2 tbsp olive oil, plus extra for greasing
1 tsp sea salt
black pepper

Time check

Prep: 20 minutes
Cooking: 30 minutes

White bean and rosemary dip with tortilla crisps

I do love a dip and this one is so quick and easy to make. Makes a great snack or starter with the tortilla crisps and some raw veggies, such as carrot and cucumber sticks and lovely red radishes.

1 For the dip, heat the olive oil in a medium saucepan and add the garlic and rosemary (set aside a little chopped rosemary for garnishing). Heat the oil gently for 30 seconds or until the mixture smells fragrant but the garlic isn't coloured, then remove the pan from the heat.

2 Tip the beans into a food processor, add the oil, garlic and rosemary mixture and 2–3 tablespoons of water. Season with salt and pepper and blend until you have the consistency you prefer. I like this dip to have a bit of texture – not too smooth.

3 Spoon the dip into a serving dish, drizzle with a little more oil and a sprinkling of chopped rosemary.

4 For the tortilla crisps, preheat the oven to 180°C/Fan 160°C/Gas 4. Cut the tortillas into triangles, brush or spray them with a little oil, then season with salt and paprika. Place them in a single layer on a baking tray and bake for 3 minutes or until just golden and crisp. Turn them over, sprinkle with a little more paprika and bake for another 2 minutes or until golden and crisp.

5 Sprinkle the hot crisps with chopped rosemary and serve them with the dip and some raw veggies.

Serves 4
249 calories per serving

2 tbsp olive oil, plus extra for drizzling
2 garlic cloves, chopped
1 large sprig of rosemary, leaves stripped and chopped
2 x 400g cans of cannellini beans, drained and rinsed
salt and black pepper

Tortilla crisps
4 corn tortillas
1–2 tbsp olive oil or light spray oil
½ tsp smoked paprika
1 tsp chopped fresh rosemary leaves

Time check

Prep: 10 minutes
Cooking: 5 minutes

Sesame kale crisps

We all need a little crunchy, salty something to snack on sometimes and these are no trouble to make – they disappear in moments! They don't keep well and are best eaten on the day, so divide the recipe in half if you don't want so many.

1 Preheat the oven to 200°C/Fan 180°C/Gas 6.

2 Remove the tough stems of the kale and discard them, then tear the leaves into roughly 3cm pieces. Place them on a couple of large shallow baking trays.

3 Drizzle the sesame oil over the leaves and massage it in with your hands. Sprinkle the leaves with coarse sea salt.

4 Put the trays in the oven and roast the leaves for 8–10 minutes or until crisp. Shake the trays occasionally to make sure the kale cooks evenly. Sprinkle the crisps with sesame seeds and serve them straight away while they're still warm.

Serves 6
118 calories per serving

200g kale
2 tbsp sesame oil
2 tbsp sesame seeds
sea salt

Time check

Prep: 2 minutes
Cooking: 15 minutes

Seedy soda bread

This will keep for two or three days wrapped in foil. But if you don't want to eat it all in that time, slice the bread, wrap the slices tightly in baking paper and foil, then freeze them. You can pop slices in the toaster as you need them – a speedy way to a snack.

1 Preheat the oven to 190°C/Fan 170°C/Gas 5. Line a baking tray with baking paper.

2 Sift the flours and bicarbonate of soda into a large bowl. Add the salt, oats and seeds (reserving a tablespoon of seeds for later) and mix everything together.

3 Crack the egg into a measuring jug, add the buttermilk and whisk. Make a well in the middle of the dry ingredients and then gradually add the liquid, stirring with a wooden spoon until it comes together into a ball.

4 Finish shaping the loaf into a ball with your hands, using extra flour to stop the dough sticking if you need to. Place the loaf on the baking tray and cut a cross in the top. Brush the loaf with milk and scatter over the reserved seeds.

5 Bake the loaf in the preheated oven for 30–35 minutes or until it is pale golden and sounds hollow when you tap the bottom. Serve warm with butter.

Makes 1 loaf (about 10 slices)
177 calories per slice

200g spelt flour, plus extra for dusting
100g wholemeal or rye flour
1 tsp bicarbonate of soda
1 tsp salt
50g rolled oats
50g mixed seeds (sunflower, pumpkin and sesame)
1 large egg
1 x 284ml carton of buttermilk
1 tbsp milk

Time check

Prep: 10 minutes
Cooking: 35 minutes

Nut butters

I didn't think I was the sort of person who could make my own nut butter, but you just won't believe how easy it is! And it's way cheaper than the bought stuff. It's great to get the kids into the habit of having home-made nut butter as a snack on toast or crackers instead of sugary jams and spreads. Use almonds, hazelnuts or cashews or a mixture, add seeds – whatever you fancy.

1 Preheat the oven to 150°C/Fan 130°C/Gas 2. Place the nuts in a single layer on a large shallow baking tray, add a pinch of sea salt and roast them for 10–15 minutes.

2 Tip the roasted nuts into a high-powered food processor and blitz. You'll probably need to process the nuts for about 10 minutes until the natural oils start coming out. Stop every couple of minutes to scrape down the sides and keep blitzing until the mix is smooth and creamy.

3 Spoon the nut butter into a jar and seal. It will keep well in the fridge for up to 3 weeks.

Davina's tip

You can use skinned or unskinned nuts. In fact, unskinned nuts, particularly almonds, are even better for you as the skins contain extra nutrients. The butter may be darker and flecked with bits of skin but it is still delicious.

Makes 300g

60 calories per 10g serving

300g unsalted nuts, such as
    hazelnuts, almonds or cashews
pinch of sea salt

Time check

Prep: 10 minutes
Cooking: 10–15 minutes

Giant crispbreads

My super-sized crispbreads will keep for two weeks in a sealed container and they're perfect served with any kind of dip, such as the white bean dip (see page 141) or the spicy squash hummus (see page 137). You can vary the flavourings and add dried chilli, poppy and sesame seeds, thyme, fennel seeds – whatever you fancy. You will need two baking trays for cooking these – they really are mahoosive.

1 Preheat the oven to 200°C/Fan 180°C/Gas 6. Measure 125ml of warm water into a measuring jug and sprinkle over the yeast. Add the oil and whisk together with a fork. Cover the jug with a tea towel and leave the yeast to froth up for 5 minutes.

2 Sift the flours into a large bowl and add the salt and some freshly ground black pepper. Make a well in the middle and gradually pour in the yeast mixture. Mix into a dough.

3 Lightly dust the work surface with a little flour, tip the dough out and knead it for 5 minutes or until smooth and not sticky. Put the dough back in the bowl and leave it for 15 minutes. Mix the oats, seeds and rosemary in a bowl.

4 Cut the dough into 4 equal balls. Cut 2 pieces of baking paper the same size as your baking trays. Dust 1 of the pieces of paper with flour, place a ball of dough on to it and roll it out into a round, making it as thin as possible. Sprinkle with a quarter of the oats, mixed seeds, cumin seeds and rosemary and roll again to press the seeds into the dough. Repeat to make another crispbread. Place the crispbreads (still on the baking paper) on to the baking trays and bake for 10–15 minutes or until golden and crisp.

5 Repeat with the rest of dough and mixture. Break the crispbreads into pieces and serve them with dips and raw vegetables.

Makes 4 large crispbreads (each is at least 2 servings)

140 calories per serving

7g packet fast-action yeast
1 tbsp extra virgin olive oil
100g wholemeal spelt flour
100g wholemeal or rye flour, plus
  extra for rolling
1 tsp sea salt
2 tbsp porridge oats
2 tbsp mixed seeds
1 tsp cumin seeds
1 tbsp chopped rosemary
salt and black pepper

Time check

Prep: 20 minutes
Cooking: 20 minutes

Warm anchovy dip

Most dips are cold so it's a nice change to have a warm one like this. I didn't think I liked anchovies but the flavour here is very subtle and savoury. Good served with the carrot and seed crackers on page 138 or with lots of raw veggies. Snack heaven.

1 Chop the anchovies and put them in a small saucepan with the butter and garlic. Place the pan over a low heat and stir until the butter has melted. Add the parsley and cayenne and cook for another minute.

2 Add the crème fraiche and slowly bring the mixture to the boil. Reduce the heat and simmer gently for 5–6 minutes or until reduced and thickened. Take the pan off the heat and use a stick blender to blend the mixture until smooth.

3 Pour the dip into a serving bowl and drizzle with a little of the reserved oil from the anchovies. Serve the dip warm with crackers or sticks of raw carrot, peppers and other vegetables.

Serves 8
120 calories per serving

5 anchovy fillets in olive oil, drained
    and oil reserved
25g butter
2 garlic cloves, finely chopped
1 tbsp chopped parsley
pinch of cayenne pepper
200ml crème fraiche

Time check

Prep: 5 minutes
Cooking: 10 minutes

Apple and cheese scones

Nothing makes a kitchen more homey than the smell of scones baking in the oven and they are easier to make than you think. Something I've learned is that it's much easier to cut out the scones if you dip the cutter into some flour in between each cut. This makes the cut smoother and not at all sticky and so ensures that the scones rise nice and evenly. Clever isn't it?

1 Preheat the oven to 200°C/Fan 180°C/Gas 6. Line a baking tray with baking paper. Put the flour, baking powder and butter in a food processor and blitz until the mixture resembles fine breadcrumbs, then tip it into a bowl.

2 Grate the apple into a clean tea towel, then squeeze out as much liquid as you can – it's important to do this, otherwise the mixture will be too sticky. Stir the apple into the flour mixture, then add the herbs and half the cheese and season well.

3 Crack the egg into a measuring jug and whisk in enough of the buttermilk to make it up to 150ml. Stir in the mustard. Make a well in the centre of the flour and apple mixture, pour in the egg and milk and bring everything together with a spoon to form a soft dough.

4 Transfer the dough to a lightly floured work surface and knead it briefly to bring it together into a ball. Using a rolling pin, roll out the dough to a thickness of about 3cm. With a 5cm straight-sided pastry cutter, cut out 12 scones, rerolling the dough as necessary. Place the scones on the baking tray, spacing them well apart. Brush the tops with any remaining buttermilk and scatter with the rest of the cheese.

5 Bake the scones for 12–15 minutes or until they're well risen and light golden in colour. Remove them from the oven and leave them to cool on a wire rack, then serve warm. They're yummily wonderful split in half and spread with a little butter and served with a few slices of cheese and apple on the side.

Davina's tip

These are best eaten the day you make them so if you don't need them all, pack them into a freezer-proof container once cool and freeze them for up to 1 month. Defrost the scones and warm them through in the oven before serving.

Makes 12

195 calories per scone

300g spelt flour, plus extra for rolling
2 tsp baking powder
75g butter, chilled and diced
1 apple, such as Cox or Braeburn
2 sprigs of rosemary, leaves picked and finely chopped or 6 sprigs of fresh thyme, stalks discarded
125g extra-mature Cheddar cheese, grated
1 egg
about 125ml buttermilk
2 tsp grainy mustard
salt and black pepper

Time check

Prep: 10 minutes
Cooking: 15 minutes

Prune and almond chocolate truffles

I just love these and although they are rich and sweet, they contain lots of good things. They look so fancy too with the dark chocolate coating. Don't be tempted to eat too many though – they are scarily moreish!

1 Preheat the oven to 200°/Fan 180°C/Gas 6. Spread the almonds or hazelnuts on a baking tray and pop them in the oven for 8–10 minutes until golden.

2 Place the dates, prunes and 100g of the toasted nuts into a food processor and blitz them until finely chopped. Add the cocoa powder, honey and almond butter or olive oil and process again until combined.

3 Roll the mixture into small bite-size balls slightly smaller than a walnut. Place them on a tray lined with baking paper and pop them in the fridge to chill for 5 minutes while you melt the chocolate.

4 Melt the chocolate in a bowl set over a pan of simmering water – don't allow the bottom of the bowl to touch the water – or in the microwave in short bursts. Finely chop the rest of the nuts.

5 Stick a cocktail stick into each ball, dip it in the melted chocolate and then place it on a wire rack. Sprinkle some of the truffles with the chopped nuts and dust the rest with sifted cocoa powder or leave them plain.

6 Leave the truffles to set for 15–20 minutes in the fridge before serving them.

P.S. Go on, have a go – these are way easier than you think and you're totally going to love them!

Makes 24

87 calories per truffle

130g blanched almonds or hazelnuts
75g medjool or soft dates, pitted
125g soft pitted prunes
3 tbsp cocoa powder, plus extra
   for dusting
1 tbsp runny honey
2 tbsp smooth almond butter or light
   olive oil
85g dark chocolate, 70% cocoa
   content, broken into squares

Time check

Prep: 10 minutes,
   plus chilling time
Cooking: 10 minutes

Chocolate, cherry and almond fudge

This is a naughty little treat to have in the freezer for when you get that irresistible urge for something sweet. You can leave out the almonds and cherries if you want something plainer or you can add other dried fruit or nuts, such as sultanas, dried apricots, hazelnuts, pecans and so on. Medjool dates do add a fab flavour but you can also use soft pitted dates which are cheaper. The fudge can be kept in the freezer for up to three months – if you're really strong-willed!

1 Put the dates in a saucepan and add enough boiling water to cover them. Place the pan over a medium heat and simmer the dates gently for about 5 minutes or until they are really soft.

2 Meanwhile, toast the almonds, if using, for about 5 minutes in a dry frying pan over a low heat. Set them aside to cool slightly, then chop them roughly.

3 Tip the dates into a sieve to drain and discard the water. Transfer the dates to a food processor and leave them to cool for a few minutes. Add the nut butter, butter, maple syrup and cocoa powder and blend until smooth. Stir in the chopped nuts and dried cherries, if using.

4 Lightly grease a 25cm square shallow baking tray and line it with baking paper. Spoon the mixture into the tray and spread the surface flat with a spatula. Cover with another layer of baking paper and put the fudge in the freezer for 3 hours to set.

5 Remove the fudge from the freezer and let it defrost for 5 minutes before cutting it into small squares. Put the squares in a freezer-proof container and keep them in the freezer until needed. Allow the fudge to defrost for 5 minutes before you eat it.

Makes 20 pieces

137 calories per piece

400g medjool or soft dates, pitted
50g blanched almonds (optional)
200g smooth nut butter (almond is
    good)
60g butter
1 tbsp maple syrup
3 tbsp cocoa powder
50g sour dried cherries (optional)

Time check

Prep: 15 minutes,
    plus freezing time
Cooking: 5 minutes

Fruit and nut cookies

I avoid sugar-packed bought biscuits nowadays, but I do like to make these which are just sweetened with a little apple juice and are completely yummy. To save time, look for packets of ready-roasted nuts. If you can't find any, just scatter plain unsalted nuts on a shallow baking tray and roast them for 10 minutes in a preheated oven (200°C/Fan 180°C/Gas 6).

1 First toast the pumpkin seeds and sesame seeds separately in a dry pan until they're lightly golden and smelling fragrant. Line a baking tray with baking paper.

2 Preheat the oven to 180°C/Fan 160°C/Gas 4. Place the nuts, dried fruit, toasted pumpkin seeds, 2 tablespoons of the toasted sesame seeds, the chia seeds and the coconut into a blender or food processor and pulse until roughly chopped. Then gradually add the apple juice to make a soft dough.

3 Roll the mixture into 20 walnut-size balls and place them on the lined baking tray, then press each one with your fingers to flatten slightly. Sprinkle over the remaining sesame seeds and a little desiccated coconut, or some sunflower seeds – a mix of all of these makes a pretty collection of biscuits.

4 Bake the biscuits for 20 minutes or until golden brown. Leave them to cool for 5 minutes on the baking tray, then transfer them to a wire rack. Once they are completely cool, the biscuits can be stored in a sealed container for 3 or 4 days.

Makes 20
142 calories per cookie

1 tbsp pumpkin seeds
3 tbsp sesame seeds
200g mixed unsalted roasted nuts (almonds, pecans or hazelnuts)
175g mixed dried fruit (prunes, apricots, cherries or figs)
2 tbsp chia seeds
75g desiccated coconut, plus extra for sprinkling
6–7 tbsp unsweetened apple juice
1 tbsp sunflower seeds, for decorating

Time check

Prep: 15 minutes
Cooking: 20 minutes

Smoothies

I never tire of smoothies and I'm always up for new combos. These all work in a blender, but the high-powered gadgets you can get do make a smoother smoothie.

Green pineapple smoothie

Frozen pineapple is perfect for smoothies and you don't have to fiddle about chopping and removing those spiky bits. Just put everything in a blender and blitz until smooth. Pour the mixture into a chilled glass and drink straight away.

Time check

Prep: 5 minutes
Cooking: 0 minutes

Serves 1

225 calories per serving

75g frozen pineapple cubes
large handful of spinach
small handful of fresh mint leaves
200ml almond milk
2 tbsp plain yoghurt
1 tsp honey
1 tbsp milled seeds (flaxseeds,
    linseeds, sunflower and/or
    pumpkin seeds)

Watermelon, strawberry and mint smoothie

This is so simple and refreshing. Place all the ingredients in a blender and blitz until smooth. Pour the mixture into a chilled glass and serve immediately.

Time check

Prep: 5 minutes
Cooking: 0 minutes

Serves 1

68 calories per serving

125g watermelon, skin and seeds
    removed (peeled weight)
75g strawberries, hulled
small handful of fresh mint leaves
150ml cold water
squeeze of fresh lime juice, to taste
handful of ice

Banana, blueberry and oat smoothie

The seeds in this add loads of extra goodness. It's best to use the milled sort unless you have a really high-powered blender that can break down whole seeds. Just put everything in a blender and blitz until smooth. Pour the mixture into a chilled glass and drink it straight away.

Time check

Prep: 5 minutes
Cooking: 0 minutes

Serves 1

328 calories per serving

65g blueberries
1 small banana, chopped
1 tbsp Greek yoghurt (optional)
2 tsp milled flaxseeds or a mix of
   milled seeds and nuts
15g porridge oats
150ml milk or almond milk

Berrytastic smoothie

Don't be scared of the beetroot – you can hardly taste it and it adds loads of vitamins and minerals. Put everything in a blender and blitz until smooth – add extra water if it's too thick. Pour the mixture into a chilled glass and drink straight away.

Time check

Prep: 5 minutes
Cooking: 0 minutes

Serves 1

219 calories per serving

75g raw beetroot, chopped
100g mixed frozen berries
1 tbsp natural yoghurt
2 tsp runny honey or to taste
1 tbsp almond butter
200ml cold water

−6−

sweet Things

Raspberry, coconut and lime panna cotta 167

Strawberry cheesecake 168

Watermelon, pomegranate and mint granita 171

Chargrilled peaches with orange cream 172

Chocolate, honey and raspberry parfait 175

Drop scones with fresh berries 176

Frozen chocolate banana popsicles 179

Blackcurrant and mint sorbet 180

Banana, oat and sultana muffins 183

Carrot, apple and walnut cupcakes 184

Chocolate, beetroot and hazelnut tray bake 187

Coffee and walnut tray bake 188

Courgette, lemon and poppy seed cake 191

Fruity flapjacks 192

Lemon drizzle cake 195

Squidgy banana and pecan tray bake 196

Malt loaf 199

Sticky gingerbread 200

Sweet potato and pecan brownies 203

Raspberry, coconut and lime panna cotta

When working on my first cookbook I discovered how to make panna cotta and now there's no stopping me. There's no refined sugar in these – just honey and the natural sweetness of coconut milk – and they are truly divine. Wibbly, wobbly deliciousness.

1 Place the gelatine sheets in a bowl, cover them with cold water and leave them to soften for 5 minutes.

2 Pour the cream, coconut milk, honey and lime zest and juice into a small saucepan. Gently bring the mixture to the boil over a low heat, then remove the pan from the heat. Squeeze the gelatine to remove any excess water, then add it to the hot cream mix and stir well until completely melted.

3 Lightly oil 4 moulds or ramekins. Divide the mixture between them and leave them in the fridge for at least 4 hours or until completely set.

4 To make the coulis, put the raspberries and honey in a blender and blend until smooth. Pass the mixture through a sieve into a small jug.

5 To serve, dip the moulds into very hot water for a few seconds, then turn the panna cottas out on to plates. Pour a little coulis over the top of each panna cotta and serve with fresh raspberries.

Serves 4
393 calories per serving

4 sheets of leaf gelatine
100ml double cream
400ml coconut milk
50ml honey
finely grated zest of 1 lime and juice
   of ½ lime
oil, for greasing

Raspberry coulis
200g raspberries, plus extra to serve
3–4 tbsp runny honey

Time check

Prep: 15 minutes,
   plus chilling time
Cooking: 10 minutes

Strawberry cheesecake

I used to make my cheesecake base with shop-bought biscuits, but they all contain loads of refined sugar, so I find that this oatcake version is a godsend – and it tastes good too. The rest is a doddle and it is beyond gorgeous for an occasional treat. Ideally, leave the cheesecake to chill overnight in the fridge so it is properly set when you serve it.

1 Start by making the base. Put the oatcakes in a blender and blitz until they resemble breadcrumbs. Melt the butter with the honey and vanilla in a small pan, add the crushed oatcakes and mix everything together well.

2 Lightly grease a 20cm loose-bottomed springform cake tin. Spoon the oatcake mixture into the base of the tin and press it down with a potato masher to make an even layer. Pop it in the fridge to chill while you make the topping.

3 Put the cream cheese, honey, half the orange zest, the vanilla and yoghurt into a blender and blitz until smooth. Add 200g of the strawberries and blitz a few times until they're coarsely chopped. Pour the strawberry mixture over the top of the oatcake base and smooth the surface. Chill for 3 hours or ideally overnight.

4 To serve, decorate the top with the remaining strawberries and grated orange zest and cut into wedges.

Davina's tip

I always used to use vanilla extract in cakes and puds, but it does contain sugar so then I found that vanilla pods weren't as scary as I thought and got into the habit of using them. Now I've also discovered vanilla powder, which is really easy. It seems a bit pricy but a tub does last for ages. Up to you.

Serves 8
400 calories per serving

400g full-fat cream cheese
3 tbsp orange blossom honey
finely grated zest of 1 orange
seeds scraped from 1 vanilla pod
    or 1 tsp vanilla powder
100g Greek yoghurt
400g strawberries, hulled and
    quartered

Base
200g oatcakes
75g butter, plus extra for greasing
75g orange blossom honey
1 tsp vanilla powder

Time check

Prep: 20 minutes, plus chilling
Cooking: 5 minutes

Watermelon, pomegranate and mint granita

You don't need to add any honey or other sweetness to this as the watermelon is lovely and sweet already. When you're squeezing the lime, you'll get some little flecks of lime flesh in the juice – leave these in as they add a nice sharpness to the mixture which is very refreshing. This makes plenty but it keeps well in the freezer.

1 Put the watermelon flesh in a blender with most of mint – reserve some nice sprigs to garnish the granita. Blitz until the watermelon has broken down.

2 Pour the mixture through a fine sieve directly into a plastic freezer-proof container to remove the melon seeds. Pour in the pomegranate juice and the lime juice and flesh.

3 Cover the container with a lid and place it in the freezer. As the mixture freezes, scrape it with a fork every 2 hours to break up and disperse the ice crystals.

4 Serve in scoops with extra mint sprigs and pomegranate seeds scattered over the top.

Serves 8
55 calories per serving

600g watermelon, cut into cubes
small handful of fresh mint leaves, stems discarded, plus extra to serve
100ml unsweetened fresh pomegranate juice
juice of 1 lime
25g pomegranate seeds, to serve

Time check

Prep: 15 minutes, plus freezing time
Cooking: 0 minutes

Chargrilled peaches with orange cream

Grilling peaches does something magical to their flavour, and the orange and vanilla cream is a perfect accompaniment to the fragrant fruit. You can prepare this dish ahead of time if you like and just warm the peaches in the oven for a few minutes before serving.

1 Toast the almonds in a dry pan until they're lightly golden, then set them aside.

2 Heat a griddle pan until smoking hot. Brush the cut side of the peaches with oil. Add the peaches to the griddle and grill them for 2–3 minutes on each side or until lightly charred and just tender – you might need to do this in batches. Transfer the peaches to a serving dish as they are cooked.

3 Drizzle the grilled peaches with a tablespoon of the maple syrup and most of the orange juice (save a tablespoon for adding to the cream), then scatter with half the orange zest.

4 In a bowl, whip the cream until it forms soft peaks, then add the yoghurt, vanilla seeds or powder, and the rest of the maple syrup, orange juice and zest.

5 Serve the peaches warm, adding a sprinkling of toasted flaked almonds and a generous dollop of the orange and vanilla cream.

Serves 4
309 calories per serving

40g flaked almonds, to garnish
4 large ripe peaches, halved and
    stones removed (white fleshed ones
    are the best!)
1 tsp groundnut or light olive oil
2 tbsp maple syrup
juice and finely grated zest of
    1 orange
100ml whipping cream
100ml Greek yoghurt
seeds scraped from 1 vanilla pod or
    1 tsp vanilla powder

Time check

Prep: 10 minutes
Cooking: 10 minutes

Chocolate, honey and raspberry parfait

This is totally amazing, takes minutes to put together and doesn't need cooking. Just pop it in the freezer and take it out ten minutes before you are ready to serve so it softens slightly and you can slice it easily. Yum. The parfait is equally fab with fresh cherries when they're in season, but make sure you remove the stones!

1 Lightly oil a 9 x 19cm loaf tin and line the base with a strip of baking paper that's long enough to stick up at each end of the tin. Oil the paper too. Now line the loaf tin with cling film, leaving enough to fold over the top of the parfait – this will make it much easier to remove the parfait from the tin later.

2 Whip the double cream with the vanilla seeds until it forms soft peaks, then fold in the Greek yoghurt, honey and orange zest. Fold in the chopped chocolate (reserving a little to garnish the parfait later) and the raspberries.

3 Spoon the mixture into the prepared tin, fold the cling film over the top and freeze until solid – about 2 hours or a maximum of 4 hours.

4 To turn out the parfait, remove it from the freezer and let it defrost for 10 minutes. Pull the strip of baking paper, which should help release the parfait from the tin, then invert it on to a serving plate and peel off the cling film. Top with a drizzle of honey and extra raspberries and the reserved chocolate, then cut into slices to serve.

Davina's tip

If you have trouble turning out the parfait, run a hot cloth along the outside of the tin to help release it.

**Makes 1 parfait
(10 slices)**

220 calories per slice

oil, for greasing
300ml double cream
seeds scraped from 1 vanilla pod
200ml Greek yoghurt
2 tbsp orange blossom honey or
    heather honey, plus extra for
    drizzling
finely grated zest of ½ orange
75g dark chocolate, chopped
150g fresh raspberries
extra honey and raspberries, to serve

Time check

Prep: 10 minutes,
    plus freezing time
Cooking: 0 minutes

Drop scones with fresh berries

One word: yum. These are *so* quick and easy to prepare and make a lovely little teatime treat on a Sunday afternoon.

1 Sift the flour, baking powder and salt into a bowl and mix them together. Measure the milk into a jug and crack in the egg, then add the honey and vanilla and whisk together.

2 Make a well in the middle of the dry mixture and gradually add the liquid. Whisk continuously until it is all incorporated and the batter is thick and smooth.

3 Heat a non-stick frying pan, add a dot of butter and swirl it around to melt it. Spoon 4 tablespoonfuls of the batter into the pan, spacing them well apart – this will make drop scones measuring about 6cm across. As soon as bubbles appear on the surface of the scones, flip them over and cook them on the other side until puffed in the middle.

4 Remove the scones, put them on a plate and cover to keep them warm while you cook the rest. Wipe out the pan with kitchen paper and add fresh butter for each batch.

5 Serve topped with fresh berries and a drizzle of honey if you like.

Makes about 20

47 calories per scone

140g wholemeal spelt flour
2 tsp baking powder
pinch of fine salt
150ml whole milk
1 large egg
1 tbsp runny honey, plus extra
    to serve
seeds scraped from 1 vanilla pod or
    1 tsp vanilla powder
25g butter
fresh berries, to serve

Time check

Prep: 5 minutes
Cooking: 10 minutes

Frozen chocolate banana popsicles

This is a bit of magic: because the bananas are frozen, the chocolate sets almost immediately when you dip the bananas into it. They're great fun for children, who love the dipping and coating, and they're much healthier than your usual ice lollies. You can make them so look so pretty too.

1 Peel the bananas and cut each one in half across the middle. Place a lolly stick or a short wooden skewer into the middle of each banana, place them on a tray and freeze them for 1 hour or until solid.

2 Meanwhile, put the chocolate, honey and oil in a bowl that fits snugly over a pan of gently simmering water. The bottom of the bowl shouldn't touch the water. Stir occasionally until the chocolate has melted.

3 Quickly dip the frozen bananas into the melted chocolate so that they are covered all over and then sprinkle them with your choice of nuts, coconut or raspberries. Serve immediately.

Davina's tip

If you want more of these little treats, just double or treble the recipe.

Serves 4

224 calories per serving

2 ripe bananas
75g dark chocolate, broken into
    squares
2 tsp honey
1 tbsp hazelnut or light olive oil
2 tbsp chopped toasted hazelnuts,
    nibbed pistachios, almonds,
    unsweetened desiccated coconut or
    freeze-dried raspberry pieces

Time check

Prep: 5 minutes,
    plus freezing time
Cooking: 5 minutes

Blackcurrant and mint sorbet

Blackcurrants have a short season but they have such an amazing flavour and are very rich in vitamin C so I like to enjoy them whenever I can. It's well worth making this sorbet when blackcurrants are in the shops and stashing it away in the freezer, ready to cheer up a winter supper. If you can't get blackcurrants you could use those packs of frozen mixed berries you find in the supermarket.

1 Pour the honey into a saucepan and add 200ml of just-boiled water and the mint. Put a lid on the pan and bring the water and honey to the boil, then turn down the heat and simmer for 5 minutes. Add the blackcurrants, cover the pan again and simmer for 5 minutes or until all the blackcurrants have popped.

2 Pour everything into a food processor and blend a few times. Tip the mixture into a sieve placed over a bowl and push it through, extracting as much of the juice as you can. Discard the blackcurrant skins and mint sprigs left in the sieve. Stir in the lemon juice and leave the liquid to cool completely.

3 Once the liquid is cool, transfer it to an ice cream maker and churn for about 10–15 minutes or until the sorbet starts to form. Transfer it to a freezer-proof container with a lid and freeze for at least 2 hours prior to serving. If you don't have an ice cream maker, freeze and beat the mixture 3 or 4 times as it freezes.

4 To serve, scoop spoonfuls of sorbet into bowls and garnish with a sprig of mint.

Serves 4

200 calories per serving

175ml honey
large handful of fresh mint, plus extra sprigs to serve
750g fresh blackcurrants, stems removed
4 tbsp fresh lemon juice

Time check

Prep: 10 minutes, plus churning and freezing
Cooking: 10 minutes

Banana, oat and sultana muffins

These are perfect for a breakfast on the go or a snack for the children and their friends after school. They're best eaten the day they're made, but you can pop some in the freezer for another time. Just warm them through slightly after defrosting.

1 Preheat the oven to 180°C/Fan 160°C/Gas 4 and line a muffin tin with paper cases.

2 Sift the flour, bicarb and salt into a large bowl, then add the vanilla and stir in 50g of the oats (save the rest for later). Set half a banana aside, then in a separate bowl, mash the remaining 1½ bananas until smooth. Stir the honey, buttermilk, oil and eggs into the mashed bananas and mix everything together.

3 Make a well in the centre of the dry ingredients. Pour the banana mixture into the well and stir with a wooden spoon until everything just comes together. Fold in the sultanas. Divide the mix evenly between the muffin cases and smooth the tops to flatten.

4 Cut the reserved banana half into 12 slices and place a slice on top of each muffin. Sprinkle the tops with the rest of the oats and drizzle with a little honey.

5 Bake the muffins for 18–20 minutes or until they have risen and are golden. Leave them to cool for 5 minutes in the tin, then transfer them to a wire rack to cool completely.

Makes 12
224 calories per muffin

300g wholemeal spelt flour
1 tsp bicarbonate of soda
pinch of salt
seeds scraped from 1 vanilla pod or
    1 tsp vanilla powder
60g porridge oats
2 ripe bananas
125g runny honey, plus a little extra
    for drizzling
284ml buttermilk
3 tbsp light olive oil
2 eggs
100g sultanas

Time check

Prep: 10 minutes
Cooking: 18–20 minutes

Carrot, apple and walnut cupcakes

Chopping the apple rather than grating it does take an extra minute or two but it is well worth it. You get lovely little nuggets of apple as you bite into the cupcake. Icing is optional – looks pretty but it does add calories of course.

1 Preheat the oven to 180°C/Fan 160°C/Gas 4. Line a 12-hole cupcake tin with paper cases.

2 Put the grated carrot in a large bowl. Add the apple (reserving some to garnish), cinnamon, orange zest, walnuts, if using, and the honey. Add a pinch of salt, the oil and the eggs and whisk together. Sift the flour, baking powder and bicarb into the bowl and fold them in until the mixture is well combined.

3 Divide the mixture between the paper cases and smooth the top with a spatula, then scatter over the reserved apple pieces.

4 Bake the cupcakes for 15–18 minutes, or until risen and springy to the touch. Remove them from the oven and leave them in the tin for 5 minutes, then place them on a wire rack to cool completely.

5 For the icing, if using, beat the butter and cream cheese together until light and fluffy. Beat in the maple syrup and orange zest. Once the cupcakes are cool, spread them with the icing, place a walnut on top of each and scatter with a little orange zest.

Makes 12

160 calories per cake

251 calories per cake with icing

100g finely grated carrot
1 apple, cored and cut into small cubes (about 125g)
1 tsp ground cinnamon
finely grated zest of 1 orange
50g walnuts, chopped (optional)
100g runny honey
pinch of salt
85ml light olive oil
2 eggs, beaten
125g self-raising wholemeal flour
½ tsp baking powder
½ tsp bicarbonate of soda

Icing (optional)
50g butter, softened
150g soft cream cheese, at room temperature
2 tbsp maple syrup
finely grated zest of 1 orange, plus extra to decorate
12 walnut halves

Time check

Prep: 20 minutes
Cooking: 18 minutes

Chocolate, beetroot and hazelnut tray bake

Hmm – chocolate and beetroot? Can this work? The answer is yes, it really can and it does – deliciously. The beetroot adds a lovely juiciness and richness to the mixture and the cake doesn't taste beetrooty at all. But, although this contains beetroot, remember that it is still a cake and high in calories so don't be tempted to have more than one square at a time. That's easier said than done – these are squidgy chocolate heaven!

1 Preheat the oven to 170°C/Fan 150°C/Gas 3½. Grease a 20cm square brownie tin with a little oil and line it with baking paper.

2 Sift all the dry ingredients into a bowl and add the vanilla. Pour the oil into a separate bowl, add the honey and malt extract and beat until well mixed. Add the eggs, one at a time, beating well in between each addition. Fold in the dry ingredients, the grated beetroot and 50g of the chopped nuts (keep the rest for later) and spoon the mixture into the prepared tin.

3 Bake the cake on the middle shelf of the oven for an hour or until a skewer comes out clean when inserted into the middle. If it looks like it is browning too much on top, cover loosely with baking paper or foil half way through the cooking time.

4 When the cake is cooked, take it out of the oven and leave it to cool for 10 minutes in the tin, then remove it from the tin and leave it to cool on a wire rack.

5 For the icing, put all the ingredients in a bowl and beat with an electric whisk until smooth. Spread the icing over the top of the cake and decorate with the remaining chopped hazelnuts. To serve, cut it into 16 squares.

Makes 16 squares

227 calories per square
330 calories per square with icing

300ml light olive or hazelnut oil, plus extra for greasing
175g spelt flour
2 tsp baking powder
1 tsp bicarbonate of soda
2 tbsp cocoa powder
pinch of fine sea salt
seeds scraped from 1 vanilla pod or 1 tsp vanilla powder
200g runny honey
100g malt extract
3 large eggs
225g grated raw beetroot
75g hazelnuts, chopped

Icing

100g smooth hazelnut or almond butter
2 tbsp maple syrup
1½ tbsp cocoa powder
2 tbsp milk

Time check

Prep: 25 minutes
Cooking: 60 minutes

Coffee and walnut tray bake

Coffee and walnut cake is such a classic and a huge favourite of mine. I love that this is a tray bake rather than a big round cake – makes it easier to take just one little square and be happy. So good. So satisfying.

1 Preheat the oven to 170°C/Fan 150°C/Gas 3½. Lightly grease a 20cm square brownie tin with butter and line it with baking paper.

2 Measure all the cake ingredients into a large bowl and beat them with an electric whisk until combined. Pour the mixture into the prepared tin and bake for 35–40 minutes or until the sponge springs back when you press it with your finger. Take the cake out of the oven and leave it to cool on a wire rack.

3 For the icing, mix the espresso powder with a tablespoon of hot water and set it aside to cool. Put the mascarpone and maple syrup into a bowl and beat with an electric whisk until smooth. Beat in the cold coffee.

4 Remove the cake from the tin, peel off the baking paper and put it on a board. Spread the icing over the cake and decorate it with walnut halves, then cut it into 16 squares. They will keep for 2–3 days in the fridge, but take them out and allow them to come to room temperature before serving.

Makes 16 squares

211 calories per square
252 calories per square with icing

225g butter, softened, plus extra for greasing
225g runny honey
275g wholemeal spelt flour
4 tsp baking powder
4 large eggs
2 tsp instant espresso powder, mixed with 2 tbsp water or 2 tbsp strong cold coffee
75g chopped walnuts

Icing

1 tsp instant espresso powder
150g mascarpone, at room temperature
3 tbsp maple syrup
16 walnut halves

Time check

Prep: 20 minutes
Cooking: 40 minutes

Courgette, lemon and poppy seed cake

I've made cakes with carrots before but not with courgettes and was amazed – and thrilled   to find how good this is. It's light, lemony and yummy. I'm now a courgette cake convert.

1 Preheat the oven to 180°C/Fan 160°C/Gas 4. Grease 2 x 20cm loose-bottomed cake tins with oil and place a circle of baking paper in the base of each.

2 Sift all the dry ingredients into a bowl and add the vanilla. Pour the oil into a separate bowl, add the honey and beat until well mixed. Add the eggs one at a time, beating well in between each addition, then fold in the dry ingredients. Coarsely grate the courgette into a clean tea towel and squeeze well to remove the excess liquid, then add the grated courgette and the lemon zest to the mixture. Divide it evenly between the prepared tins.

3 Bake the cakes on the middle shelf of the oven for 40–45 minutes or until a skewer inserted into the middle of the cake comes out clean. If the cakes look like they are browning too much on top, cover them loosely with baking paper or foil halfway through the cooking time.

4 When the cakes are cooked, take them out of the oven and leave them to cool for 5 minutes in the tins. Remove the cakes from the tins and leave them to cool on a wire rack.

5 For the icing, whip the cream in a bowl, then fold in the mascarpone. Add the maple syrup, half the lemon zest and the lemon juice. Spread half the icing over one cake, then place the other cake on top and cover the top with the remaining icing. Scatter with the poppy seeds and the rest of the lemon zest and cut into slices to serve.

Makes a 20cm round cake (14 slices)

285 calories per slice
385 calories per slice with icing

300ml light olive oil, plus extra for
    greasing
175g spelt flour
2 tsp baking powder
1 tsp bicarbonate of soda
pinch of fine sea salt
seeds scraped from 1 vanilla pod or
    1 tsp vanilla powder
300g runny honey
3 large eggs
225g courgette
finely grated zest of 2 lemons

Icing
100ml whipping cream
200g mascarpone
3 tbsp maple syrup
finely grated zest of 1 lemon and
    2 tbsp lemon juice
1 tbsp poppy seeds

Time check

Prep: 25 minutes
Cooking: 45 minutes

Fruity flapjacks

These keep for about a week in a sealed container and make a very welcome teatime treat. They're full of good things so you needn't feel too guilty and you can cut them into nice small squares.

1 Preheat the oven to 180°C/Fan 160°C/Gas 4. Lightly grease a 20cm square tin with butter and line it with baking paper.

2 Place the dates and orange juice in a blender and blend them until smooth. Tip the blended dates into a saucepan, add the butter and honey and melt together over a low heat. Add the rest of the ingredients and stir together.

3 Scoop the mixture into the prepared tin and smooth the surface with a wooden spoon. Bake for 15–20 minutes or until golden, then remove the flapjacks from the oven and leave them to cool in the tin.

4 When the flapjacks are cool, tip them out on to a board and cut them into 16 squares.

Makes 16
165 calories per flapjack

100g butter, plus extra for greasing
150g medjool or soft dates, pitted
4 tbsp fresh orange juice
4 tbsp runny honey
50g soft dried apricots, chopped
50g sultanas
75g mixed seeds
150g rolled porridge oats

Time check

Prep: 10 minutes
Cooking: 15 minutes

Lemon drizzle cake

Okay, this cake is a bit naughty as it contains lots of butter and honey, but there's no refined sugar or white flour in it so it's definitely not as bad as regular lemon drizzle. Just make sure it is an occasional treat and limit yourself to one slice at a time and the world won't end.

1 Preheat the oven to 160°C/Fan 140°C/Gas 3. Grease a 9 x 19cm loaf tin with butter and line it with baking paper.

2 Put the butter, 165g of the honey and two-thirds of the lemon zest in a bowl and beat with an electric whisk until light and fluffy. Add the ground almonds and then the eggs, one at a time, beating well after each addition. Sift the flour and baking powder into the bowl and fold them into the mixture.

3 Spoon the mixture into the prepared tin and smooth out the top. Scatter over the flaked almonds. Bake for about 45–50 minutes, until a skewer inserted into the cake comes out clean. Take the cake out of the oven but leave it in the tin. It might sink a bit in the middle, but don't worry about that.

4 In a small pan, warm the rest of the lemon zest and the lemon juice with the remaining 50g of honey until the honey has melted. Then prick holes all over the top of the warm cake with a toothpick and gradually pour over the honey and lemon mixture. Wait for the cake to absorb one lot before adding the next. Leave the cake to cool in the tin before turning it out and cutting it into slices.

Makes 1 cake (12 slices)
254 calories per slice

175g butter, softened, plus extra for
  greasing
215g runny honey
finely grated zest of 3 unwaxed
  lemons and the juice of 1
75g ground almonds
3 eggs
100g wholemeal spelt flour
3 tsp baking powder
15g flaked almonds

Time check

Prep: 10 minutes
Cooking: 50 minutes

Squidgy banana and pecan tray bake

This is fabulously moist and delicious and takes no time at all to make. You just throw everything in the food processor, tip it into a loaf tin, then you can go off and do something useful – or not – while it bakes. You can use walnuts instead of pecans if you prefer.

1 Preheat the oven to 180°C/Fan 160°C/Gas 4. Lightly grease a 20cm square brownie tin with butter and line it with baking paper.

2 Place all the ingredients, except the pecans, into a food processor and blend until combined. Stir in the chopped pecans, keeping the whole ones for decoration.

3 Pour the mixture into the prepared tin, then decorate with some whole nuts. Bake the cake in the preheated oven for an hour or until a skewer inserted into the middle comes out clean.

4 Remove the cake from the oven and leave it to cool in the tin for 5 minutes before turning it out on to a wire rack to cool. Cut into squares to serve.

Makes 20 squares
200 calories per square

110g butter, softened, plus extra
    for greasing
200g maple syrup
4 ripe bananas, peeled
4 tbsp whole milk
1 egg, beaten
1 tsp baking powder
½ tsp bicarbonate of soda
175g ground almonds
100g buckwheat or spelt flour
1 tsp ground cinnamon
100g pecans, chopped (plus
    10 whole nuts)

Time check

Prep: 10 minutes
Cooking: 60 minutes

Malt loaf

I do love a malt loaf and this one is super quick to prepare. Once it's in the oven you can relax while it bakes, knowing you have something special to look forward to. The loaf gets better over time so if possible leave it for a day before serving as it will get stickier and more yummy! It will keep for a week in a sealed container.

1 Preheat the oven to 150°C/Fan 130°C/Gas 2. Grease an 9 x 19cm loaf tin with oil and line it with baking paper.

2 Pour the hot tea into a large bowl, add the malt extract, honey, dried fruit and orange zest and mix together. Stir in the egg, then sift over the flour, baking powder bicarbonate of soda and a pinch of salt, then stir everything together well.

3 Pour the mixture into the prepared tin and bake for 50 minutes or until the loaf is firm on top. Take the loaf out of the oven and brush the top with a little more malt extract, then leave it to cool in the tin for 5 minutes.

4 Remove the loaf from the tin, wrap it tightly in baking paper and foil and leave it to cool. This helps to make it even stickier. Slice the loaf, spread with butter and enjoy.

Makes 1 loaf (12 slices)
118 calories per slice

light olive oil, for greasing
75ml hot Earl Grey or Lady Grey tea
90g malt extract, plus extra for
    glazing
3 tbsp honey
80g soft prunes, chopped
80g sultanas
finely grated zest of 1 orange
1 large egg, beaten
125g wholemeal spelt flour
1 tsp baking powder
½ tsp bicarbonate of soda
pinch of salt

Time check
Prep: 10 minutes
Cooking: 50 minutes

Sticky gingerbread

Gingerbread reminds me of my childhood and now I love to make it with my own lot. It's extra delicious served warm from the oven, but it also keeps well in a sealed container for up to five days.

1 Preheat the oven to 180°C/Fan 160°C/Gas 4. Lightly grease a 20cm square brownie tin with butter and line it with baking paper.

2 Sift the dry ingredients into a large bowl. Put the maple syrup, malt extract and butter in a small saucepan and place over a low heat until melted. Add the prunes, apple purée and about three quarters of the chopped stem ginger, then warm everything through for a minute. Fold this mixture into the flour using a large metal spoon. Add the eggs and milk and stir everything together to combine.

3 Pour the mixture into the prepared tin and scatter the reserved stem ginger on top. Bake for 35 minutes or until a skewer comes out clean when inserted into the middle of the cake. Remove the cake from the oven and leave it to cool in the tin. Once the gingerbread is cool, cut it into squares.

Davina's tip

You can buy apple purée but it's better to make your own. Peel and chop 2 eating apples, put them in a pan with a splash of water and cover the pan with a lid. Simmer the apples for 10 minutes or until soft, then mash with a potato masher and leave to cool before using. Weigh out 125g for the cake and enjoy the rest with some yoghurt or porridge for breakfast.

Makes 20 squares

151 calories per square

125g butter, plus extra for greasing
250g wholemeal spelt flour
2 tsp ground ginger
½ tsp ground cinnamon
1 tsp bicarbonate of soda
2 tsp baking powder
pinch of salt
100g maple syrup
100g malt extract
50g soft pitted prunes, chopped
125g apple purée
4 balls of stem ginger, finely chopped
2 large eggs, beaten
100ml whole milk

Time check

Prep: 15 minutes
Cooking: 40 minutes

Sweet potato and pecan brownies

There's no such thing as a completely healthy brownie but this version, made with sweet potato and prunes, contains lots of good things and no refined sugar. Make sure you remove the brownies from the tray five minutes after they come out of the oven or they will carry on cooking and won't be all gooey like they should be!

1 Preheat the oven to 180°C/Fan 160°C/Gas 4. Lightly grease a 20cm square brownie tin with oil and line it with baking paper.

2 Place the sweet potatoes in a microwave, pierce them with a fork and bake them for 6 minutes or until they are really soft. Remove, cool slightly and then peel. If you don't have a microwave, cook the sweet potatoes in a steamer, or in a colander that fits over a saucepan, until tender. Don't boil them or they will be too wet.

3 Measure out 175g of cooked sweet potato flesh and tip it into a blender. Add the olive oil, maple syrup and pitted prunes to make a smooth purée, then add the egg and vanilla and blitz again. Set aside.

4 Sift the dry ingredients (except the pecans and chocolate) into a large bowl. Pour the sweet potato purée into the dry ingredients and mix with a wooden spoon. Fold in the chocolate chunks and then pour the mixture into the prepared brownie tin. Smooth the top, then add the pecan halves.

5 Bake in the oven for 18 minutes. Remove the brownies from the oven and leave them to cool in the tin for 5 minutes. Then cut them into squares – they're lovely eaten while still warm.

Davina's tip

You can use walnuts instead of pecans if you prefer.

Makes 20 squares

145 calories per square

100ml light olive oil, plus extra for greasing
2 medium sweet potatoes
100g maple syrup
75g prunes, pitted
1 egg
seeds scraped from 1 vanilla pod or 1 tsp vanilla powder
100g spelt flour
4 tbsp cocoa powder
1 tsp baking powder
1 tsp bicarbonate of soda
pinch of sea salt
50g dark chocolate, cut into chunks
50g pecan halves

Time check

Prep: 20 minutes
Cooking: 25 minutes

Nutritional information

The pages that follow give you nutritional details for all the recipes in this book. These are as exact as possible but may vary slightly depending on the ingredients used when you cook the dish. Figures are per serving unless otherwise specified. Optional ingredients are not included in the analysis.

Kcals refers to the calories, or energy, in food. The calorie counts here are in kcals (kilocalories). Kj (kilojoules) are just a different way of measuring energy and not something you need worry about.

Protein We need protein for the growth and repair of tissues in the body, and meat, poultry, fish, eggs, dairy, nuts and pulses are all good sources. Research suggests that protein can help you feel fuller longer.

Carbs Smart carbs – the unrefined, wholegrain, low GI carbs used in the recipes in this book – should be an important part of our diet, even when trying to lose weight

Sugar This is total sugar, which includes the natural sugars in foods such as fruit, vegetables, milk and yoghurt. It's the free sugars – sugar added to food – that we need to cut back on.

Fat The figures for fat means the total fat content, including monounsaturated and polyunsaturated fats and saturated fat. Monounsaturated fats are found in nuts and seeds, olive and rapeseed oil, and polyunsaturated fats in oily fish and vegetable oils. They are healthier types of fat but still high in calories.

Saturated fats are found in foods such as fatty cuts of meat, butter and cheese. A diet high in saturated fat has been shown to increase the risk of heart disease.

Fibre This is a substance found in plant foods that cannot be completely broken down by digestion. Foods such as fruit, vegetables, nuts, seeds and pulses, as well as cereals like wheat, rice, maize, corn and barley, all contain fibre. When cereals are refined some of the fibre is removed.

Salt This is based on the ingredients in the recipe but does not include salt added as seasoning to taste. A high salt intake is linked with high blood pressure.

The following table shows the recommended daily amount of these various nutrients for different calorie intakes. These figures are guidelines, NOT a target.

Kcals	2,500 kcals	2,000 kcals	1,400 kcals	1,200 kcals
Protein (g)	55	45	45	45
Carbs (g)	300	270	190	160
Sugar (g)	120	90	63	54
Fat (g)	90	70	49	42
Sat fat (g)	30	20	14	12
Fibre (g)	30	30	30	30
Salt (g)	6	6	6	6

Red pepper toasties
Page 19
Kcals 234
Protein (g) 7
Carbs (g) 28
Sugar (g) 6
Fat (g) 9.5
Sat fat (g) 2.5
Fibre (g) 3
Salt (g) 0.6

**Cheesy pea fritters
(per fritter)**
Page 20
Kcals 143
Protein (g) 7
Carbs (g) 14
Sugar (g) 3
Fat (g) 6
Sat fat (g) 2
Fibre (g) 2
Salt (g) 0.3

**Asparagus and dippy
eggs**
Page 23
Kcals 129
Protein (g) 11
Carbs (g) 1
Sugar (g) 1
Fat (g) 9
Sat fat (g) 3
Fibre (g) 1.5
Salt (g) 0.3

**Baked eggs
Florentine**
Page 24
Kcals 298
Protein (g) 15
Carbs (g) 4
Sugar (g) 3
Fat (g) 24
Sat fat (g) 13
Fibre (g) 2
Salt (g) 0.6

**Home-made pot
noodles**
Page 27
Kcals 331
Protein (g) 17
Carbs (g) 48
Sugar (g) 6
Fat (g) 7
Sat fat (g) 1.4
Fibre (g) 4
Salt (g) 2.4

Nutty greens
Page 28
Kcals 375
Protein (g) 12
Carbs (g) 24.5
Sugar (g) 7
Fat (g) 23.5
Sat fat (g) 4
Fibre (g) 8.5
Salt (g) 0.1

**Bean and chorizo
soup**
Page 31
Kcals 233
Protein (g) 14
Carbs (g) 19
Sugar (g) 10
Fat (g) 10
Sat fat (g) 3.5
Fibre (g) 6.5
Salt (g) 1.5

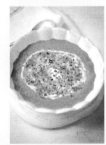

**Roasted tomato and
red pepper soup
(with goat cheese
toasts)**
Page 32
Kcals 126 (300)
Protein (g) 2.5 (8)
Carbs (g) 13 (35)
Sugar (g) 12.5 (13.5)
Fat (g) 6 (13)
Sat fat (g) 1 (4)
Fibre (g) 5 (6)
Salt (g) 0.3 (0.7)

Minty pea soup
Page 35
Kcals 216
Protein (g) 9
Carbs (g) 18
Sugar (g) 11
Fat (g) 10
Sat fat (g) 5
Fibre (g) 9
Salt (g) trace

Sunshine soup
Page 36
Kcals 337
Protein (g) 14
Carbs (g) 31
Sugar (g) 19.5
Fat (g) 15
Sat fat (g) 2.5
Fibre (g) 10
Salt (g) 0.7

Supergreen soup
Page 39
Kcals 156
Protein (g) 4.5
Carbs (g) 5
Sugar (g) 3.5
Fat (g) 12.5
Sat fat (g) 8
Fibre (g) 4
Salt (g) 0.6

**Beetroot and apple
soup**
Page 40
Kcals 172
Protein (g) 5.3
Carbs (g) 25
Sugar (g) 24
Fat (g) 4.5
Sat fat (g) 1
Fibre (g) 5.5
Salt (g) 1.5

**Cold tomato soup à
la AJ**
Page 43
Kcals 227
Protein (g) 3
Carbs (g) 13
Sugar (g) 9
Fat (g) 17
Sat fat (g) 2.5
Fibre (g) 3.5
Salt (g) 0.5

**Halloumi and
asparagus salad**
Page 47
Kcals 380
Protein (g) 16
Carbs (g) 11
Sugar (g) 4
Fat (g) 29
Sat fat (g) 11
Fibre (g) 4
Salt (g) 1.5

**Grilled corn, avocado
and feta salad**
Page 48
Kcals 281
Protein (g) 8
Carbs (g) 11
Sugar (g) 8
Fat (g) 22
Sat fat (g) 6
Fibre (g) 4
Salt (g) 1

Broccoli, spelt and orange salad
Page 51
Kcals 354
Protein (g) 10
Carbs (g) 31.5
Sugar (g) 9
Fat (g) 19
Sat fat (g) 3
Fibre (g) 8
Salt (g) 0.3

Courgette and shrimp salad
Page 52
Kcals 130
Protein (g) 10
Carbs (g) 1
Sugar (g) 9
Fat (g) 8
Sat fat (g)
Fibre (g) 1
Salt (g) 0.8

Cucumber noodle, chicken and cashew salad
Page 55
Kcals 334
Protein (g) 18
Carbs (g) 9
Sugar (g) 6
Fat (g) 24
Sat fat (g) 4
Fibre (g) 3
Salt (g) 0.3

Chicken, carrot and chickpea salad
Page 56
Kcals 342
Protein (g) 25
Carbs (g) 27
Sugar (g) 17
Fat (g) 13
Sat fat (g) 2
Fibre (g) 7
Salt (g) 0.3

Roasted beetroot and celeriac salad
Page 59
Kcals 283
Protein (g) 8
Carbs (g) 30
Sugar (g) 18
Fat (g) 13
Sat fat (g) 3.5
Fibre (g) 8
Salt (g) 0.5

Butternut and couscous salad
Page 60
Kcals 508
Protein (g) 16
Carbs (g) 78.5
Sugar (g) 29
Fat (g) 12
Sat fat (g) 2.2
Fibre (g) 13
Salt (g) 0.3

Spicy prawn salad (Spicy chicken salad)
Page 63
Kcals 173 (196)
Protein (g) 12 (15)
Carbs (g) 7 (7)
Sugar (g) 6 (6)
Fat (g) 10 (11)
Sat fat (g) 2 (2)
Fibre (g) 3 (3)
Salt (g) 1.8 (1.1)

Baked roasted tomato risotto
Page 67
Kcals 460
Protein (g) 9
Carbs (g) 66
Sugar (g) 4
Fat (g) 15
Sat fat (g) 5
Fibre (g) 3
Salt (g) 0.6

Stuffed courgettes
Page 68
Kcals 330
Protein (g) 13
Carbs (g) 34
Sugar (g) 13
Fat (g) 14
Sat fat (g) 4
Fibre (g) 5
Salt (g) 0.4

Cauliflower 'steaks' with onion and chorizo
Page 71
Kcals 285
Protein (g) 14
Carbs (g) 14
Sugar (g) 10
Fat (g) 18
Sat fat (g) 4.5
Fibre (g) 6.5
Salt (g) 1.1

Spaghetti with creamy veggie sauce
Page 72
Kcals 375
Protein (g) 11
Carbs (g) 36
Sugar (g) 5
Fat (g) 19
Sat fat (g) 9
Fibre (g) 9
Salt (g) 0.1

Cod and pesto parcels
Page 75
Kcals 265
Protein (g) 31
Carbs (g) 7
Sugar (g) 5
Fat (g) 12
Sat fat (g) 2
Fibre (g) 4.5
Salt (g) 0.6

Pan-fried lemon sole with hot tomato salsa
Page 76
Kcals 386
Protein (g) 43
Carbs (g) 10
Sugar (g) 4
Fat (g) 19
Sat fat (g) 4
Fibre (g) 3
Salt (g) 1.1

Glazed salmon with rainbow vegetables
Page 79
Kcals 516
Protein (g) 35
Carbs (g) 8
Sugar (g) 7.5
Fat (g) 36
Sat fat (g) 6
Fibre (g) 5
Salt (g) 1.5

Smoked mackerel salad with apple dressing
Page 80
Kcals 517
Protein (g) 20
Carbs (g) 15
Sugar (g) 10
Fat (g) 40
Sat fat (g) 7
Fibre (g) 4
Salt (g) 1.4

Salmon and sweet potato fishcakes
Page 83
Kcals 453
Protein (g) 23
Carbs (g) 36
Sugar (g) 15
Fat (g) 23
Sat fat (g) 4
Fibre (g) 5
Salt (g) 0.2

Grilled tuna with peppers and lentils
Page 84
Kcals 370
Protein (g) 37
Carbs (g) 17
Sugar (g) 6.5
Fat (g) 15.5
Sat fat (g) 2
Fibre (g) 6
Salt (g) 0.9

Crunchy buttermilk chicken with roasted ratatouille
Page 87
Kcals 381
Protein (g) 33
Carbs (g) 25
Sugar (g) 11.5
Fat (g) 16
Sat fat (g) 4
Fibre (g) 4
Salt (g) 0.6

Chicken Caesar salad
Page 88
Kcals 247
Protein (g) 23
Carbs (g) 13.5
Sugar (g) 2.5
Fat (g) 11
Sat fat (g) 3.5
Fibre (g) 2
Salt (g) 0.8

Lamb and apricot pilaf
Page 91
Kcals 609
Protein (g) 37
Carbs (g) 66
Sugar (g) 12
Fat (g) 20
Sat fat (g) 5
Fibre (g) 8
Salt (g) 0.2

Pork fillet with mushroom sauce
Page 92
Kcals 484
Protein (g) 35
Carbs (g) 4.5
Sugar (g) 4
Fat (g) 32
Sat fat (g) 16
Fibre (g) 1
Salt (g) 0.3

Squash 'spaghetti' with pancetta sauce
Page 95
Kcals 392
Protein (g) 12.5
Carbs (g) 28
Sugar (g) 16
Fat (g) 24
Sat fat (g) 7
Fibre (g) 7.5
Salt (g) 1.9

Seared steak with five-bean salad
Page 96
Kcals 376
Protein (g) 30
Carbs (g) 10
Sugar (g) 1
Fat (g) 22
Sat fat (g) 5
Fibre (g) 5.5
Salt (g) 0.4

Tortilla lasagne
Page 101
Kcals 416
Protein (g) 11
Carbs (g) 25
Sugar (g) 7
Fat (g) 29
Sat fat (g) 18
Fibre (g) 4.4
Salt (g) 1

Spinach and ricotta filo parcels
Page 102
Per parcel
Kcals 199
Protein (g) 5
Carbs (g) 18.5
Sugar (g) 2
Fat (g) 11
Sat fat (g) 5
Fibre (g) 2
Salt (g) 0.5

Broccoli and hot-smoked salmon tart
Page 105
Kcals 419
Protein (g) 12
Carbs (g) 9.5
Sugar (g) 2
Fat (g) 36
Sat fat (g) 20
Fibre (g) 3
Salt (g) 0.5

Fish crumble
Page 106
Kcals 354
Protein (g) 25
Carbs (g) 15
Sugar (g) 6
Fat (g) 20
Sat fat (g) 8
Fibre (g) 4.5
Salt (g) 0.7

Thai sea bass with coconut rice
Page 109
Kcals 696
Protein (g) 40
Carbs (g) 60
Sugar (g) 4
Fat (g) 28
Sat fat (g) 13.51
Fibre (g)
Salt (g) 0.3

Crispy lemon thyme chicken with roasted veggies
Page 110
Kcals 352
Protein (g) 36
Carbs (g) 17
Sugar (g) 11
Fat (g) 14
Sat fat (g) 3
Fibre (g) 7.5
Salt (g) 0.7

Chicken, leek and mushroom pie
Page 113
Kcals 569
Protein (g) 33
Carbs (g) 45
Sugar (g) 4
Fat (g) 27
Sat fat (g) 13
Fibre (g) 5
Salt (g) 1

Chicken cacciatore
Page 114
Kcals 373
Protein (g) 35
Carbs (g) 14
Sugar (g) 12/5
Fat (g) 18
Sat fat (g) 3.5
Fibre (g) 6
Salt (g) 1

Lamb casserole with Cheddar and thyme dumplings
Page 117
Kcals 571
Protein (g) 37
Carbs (g) 34
Sugar (g) 4
Fat (g) 27
Sat fat (g) 13
Fibre (g) 5
Salt (g) 1.1

Lamb kebabs with Greek salad
Page 118
Kcals 490
Protein (g) 30
Carbs (g) 8
Sugar (g) 7
Fat (g) 37
Sat fat (g) 13
Fibre (g) 4
Salt (g) 1.4

Slow-cooked pulled pork
Page 120
Kcals 349
Protein (g) 52
Carbs (g) 8
Sugar (g) 7
Fat (g) 12
Sat fat (g) 3.5
Fibre (g) 1
Salt (g) 0.4

Flatbreads
Page 121
Per flatbread
Kcals 238
Protein (g) 7.5
Carbs (g) 24
Sugar (g) 2
Fat (g) 12
Sat fat (g) 4.5
Fibre (g) 4
Salt (g) 0.1

Carrot, apple and beetroot slaw
Page 121
Kcals 230
Protein (g) 15
Carbs (g) 14.5
Sugar (g) 11
Fat (g) 17
Sat fat (g) 4
Fibre (g) 6.5
Salt (g) 0.6

Pork meatballs with pasta and tomato sauce
Page 125
Kcals 496
Protein (g) 23
Carbs (g) 46
Sugar (g) 12
Fat (g) 21
Sat fat (g) 5
Fibre (g) 9
Salt (g) 1

Slow-roast short rib ragu
Page 126
Kcals 491
Protein (g) 33
Carbs (g) 56
Sugar (g) 9
Fat (g) 11
Sat fat (g) 3
Fibre (g) 11
Salt (g) 0.4

Provençal beef casserole
Page 129
Kcals 482
Protein (g) 44
Carbs (g) 10
Sugar (g) 6
Fat (g) 20.5
Sat fat (g) 6.5
Fibre (g) 3
Salt (g) 1.5

Healthy nachos (with tomato salsa)
Page 133
Kcals 299 (399)
Protein (g) 12.5 (14)
Carbs (g) 21 (24)
Sugar (g) 1 (4)
Fat (g) 18 (27)
Sat fat (g) 9.5 (11)
Fibre (g) 1.5 (3)
Salt (g) 1.3 (1.3)

Crispy cauli cheese bites
Page 134
Kcals 256
Protein (g) 13
Carbs (g) 18
Sugar (g) 8
Fat (g) 14
Sat fat (g) 8
Fibre (g) 3
Salt (g) 0.6

Spicy squash hummus
Page 137
Kcals 204
Protein (g) 7.5
Carbs (g) 16
Sugar (g) 4.5
Fat (g) 10.5
Sat fat (g) 1.5
Fibre (g) 7.5
Salt (g) trace

Carrot and seed crackers
Page 138
Per cracker
Kcals 80
Protein (g) 3
Carbs (g) 2
Sugar (g) 1
Fat (g) 6
Sat fat (g) 1
Fibre (g) 1.2
Salt (g) 0

White bean and rosemary dip with tortilla crisps
Page 141
Kcals 249
Protein (g) 12.5
Carbs (g) 20
Sugar (g) 5
Fat (g) 11
Sat fat (g) 1.6
Fibre (g) 9
Salt (g) 0.6

Sesame kale crisps
Page 142
Kcals 118
Protein (g) 3
Carbs (g) 0.7
Sugar (g) 0.6
Fat (g) 11
Sat fat (g) 2
Fibre (g) 3
Salt (g) 0.1

Seedy soda bread
Page 145
Per slice – 10 slices
Kcals 177
Protein (g) 7.5
Carbs (g) 25
Sugar (g) 2
Fat (g) 4
Sat fat (g) 0.8
Fibre (g) 3.9
Salt (g) 0.8

Nut butters
Page 146
Per 10g serving
Kcals 60
Protein (g) 2.5
Carbs (g) 1
Sugar (g) 0.5
Fat (g) 5
Sat fat (g) 1
Fibre (g) 0.5
Salt (g) 0

Giant crispbreads
Page 149
Kcals 140
Protein (g) 4.5
Carbs (g) 18
Sugar (g) 0.4
Fat (g) 4
Sat fat (g) 0.5
Fibre (g) 3
Salt (g) 0.5

Warm anchovy dip
Page 150
Kcals 120
Protein (g) 1
Carbs (g) 0.6
Sugar (g) 0.5
Fat (g) 12.7
Sat fat (g) 8
Fibre (g) 0
Salt (g) 0.1

Apple and cheese scones
Page 153
Per scone
Kcals 195
Protein (g) 7
Carbs (g) 19
Sugar (g) 2
Fat (g) 10
Sat fat (g) 6
Fibre (g) 2.5
Salt (g) 0.9

Prune and almond chocolate truffles
Page 154
Per truffle
Kcals 87
Protein (g) 3
Carbs (g) 6
Sugar (g) 6
Fat (g) 5.5
Sat fat (g) 1
Fibre (g) 0.9
Salt (g) 0

Chocolate, cherry and almond fudge
Page 157
Per piece
Kcals 137
Protein (g) 3.5
Carbs (g) 10
Sugar (g) 8
Fat (g) 9
Sat fat (g) 2
Fibre (g) 1
Salt (g) 0.1

Fruit and nut cookies
Page 158
Per cookie
Kcals 142
Protein (g) 4
Carbs (g) 8
Sugar (g) 7
Fat (g) 10
Sat fat (g) 3
Fibre (g) 2
Salt (g) 0

Banana, blueberry and oat smoothie (Berrytastic smoothie)
Page 160
Kcals 328 (219)
Protein (g) 11 (7)
Carbs (g) 42 (25)
Sugar (g) 60 (24)
Fat (g) 12 (9)
Sat fat (g) 4 (1)
Fibre (g) 4.5 (6)
Salt (g) 0.2 (0.2)

Green pineapple smoothie (Watermelon, strawberry and mint)
Page 161
Kcals 225 (68)
Protein (g) 8 (1)
Carbs (g) 22 (13)
Sugar (g) 21 (13)
Fat (g) 11 (0)
Sat fat (g) 2 (0)
Fibre (g) 3 (3)
Salt (g) 0.4 (0)

Raspberry, coconut and lime panna cotta
Page 167
Kcals 393
Protein (g) 2.5
Carbs (g) 26
Sugar (g) 24.5
Fat (g) 31
Sat fat (g) 24
Fibre (g) 2
Salt (g) 0

Strawberry cheesecake
Page 168
Kcals 400
Protein (g) 6
Carbs (g) 33
Sugar (g) 19
Fat (g) 26
Sat fat (g) 15
Fibre (g) 4
Salt (g) 0.9

Watermelon, pomegranate and mint granita
Page 171
Kcals 55
Protein (g) 0.5
Carbs (g) 13
Sugar (g) 13
Fat (g) 0
Sat fat (g) 0
Fibre (g) 0.4
Salt (g) 0

Chargrilled peaches with orange cream
Page 172
Kcals 309
Protein (g) 6
Carbs (g) 22
Sugar (g) 21
Fat (g) 21
Sat fat (g) 9
Fibre (g) 4
Salt (g) 0.1

Chocolate, honey and raspberry parfait
Page 175
Per slice
Kcals 220
Protein (g) 2
Carbs (g) 8
Sugar (g) 8
Fat (g) 20
Sat fat (g) 12
Fibre (g) 0.7
Salt (g) 0.1

Drop scones
Page 176
Per scone
Kcals 47
Protein (g) 1.5
Carbs (g) 6
Sugar (g) 1
Fat (g) 2
Sat fat (g) 1
Fibre (g) 0.7
Salt (g) 0.2

Frozen chocolate banana popsicles
Page 179
Kcals 224
Protein (g) 3
Carbs (g) 24
Sugar (g) 23
Fat (g) 12
Sat fat (g) 4
Fibre (g) 1
Salt (g) 0

Blackcurrant and mint sorbet
Page 180
Kcals 200
Protein (g) 2
Carbs (g) 44
Sugar (g) 44
Fat (g) 0
Sat fat (g) 0
Fibre (g) 9
Salt (g) 0

Banana, oat and sultana muffins
Page 183
Per muffin
Kcals 224
Protein (g) 6
Carbs (g) 37
Sugar (g) 17
Fat (g) 5
Sat fat (g) 1
Fibre (g) 3.5
Salt (g) 0.3

Carrot, apple and walnut cupcakes
Page 184
Per cupcake (with icing)
Kcals 160 (251)
Protein (g) 3 (4.5)
Carbs (g) 15 (17)
Sugar (g) 8 (10)
Fat (g) 9 (18)
Sat fat (g) 1.5 (6)
Fibre (g) 2 (2)
Salt (g) 0.3 (0.4)

Chocolate, beetroot and hazelnut tray bake
Page 187
Per square (with icing)
Kcals 227 (330)
Protein (g) 4 (5)
Carbs (g) 23.4 (25.5)
Sugar (g) 14.5 (16.5)
Fat (g) 18 (22.5)
Sat fat (g) 2.5 (3)
Fibre (g) 1 (2)
Salt (g) 0.4 (0.4)

Coffee and walnut tray bake
Page 188
Per square (with icing)
Kcals 211 (252)
Protein (g)
Carbs (g)
Sugar (g)
Fat (g)
Sat fat (g)
Fibre (g)
Salt (g)

Courgette, lemon and poppy seed cake
Page 191
Per slice (with icing)
Kcals 285 (385)
Protein (g) 4 (5)
Carbs (g) 28 (29)
Sugar (g) 16 (19)
Fat (g) 18 (27)
Sat fat (g) 3 (9)
Fibre (g) 0.7 (0.7)
Salt (g) 0.5 (0.5)

Fruity flapjacks
Page 192
Per flapjack
Kcals 165
Protein (g) 3
Carbs (g) 19
Sugar (g) 12
Fat (g) 8
Sat fat (g) 4
Fibre (g) 2

Lemon drizzle cake
Page 195
Per slice
Kcals 254
Protein (g) 4.5
Carbs (g) 19.5
Sugar (g) 13.5
Fat (g) 17.5
Sat fat (g) 8.5
Fibre (g) 1
Salt (g) 0.6

Squidgy banana and pecan tray bake
Page 196
Per square
Kcals 200
Protein (g) 4
Carbs (g) 12
Sugar (g) 6.5
Fat (g) 15
Sat fat (g) 4
Fibre (g) 1
Salt (g) 0.2

Malt loaf
Page 199
Per slice
Kcals 118
Protein (g) 3
Carbs (g) 24
Sugar (g) 17
Fat (g) 1
Sat fat (g) 0
Fibre (g) 2
Salt (g) 0.3

Sticky gingerbread
Page 200
Per square
Kcals 151
Protein (g) 3
Carbs (g) 20
Sugar (g) 11
Fat (g) 6
Sat fat (g) 3.5
Fibre (g) 1.5
Salt (g) 0.4

Sweet potato and pecan brownies
Page 203
Per square
Kcals 145
Protein (g) 2
Carbs (g) 16.5
Sugar (g) 7.5
Fat (g) 7
Sat fat (g) 1.5
Fibre (g) 2
Salt (g) 0.3

My 5-Week Plan

I like cooking and I love eating – I don't even mind doing the shopping. But I do find that the worst thing is deciding what to cook. It's all too easy just to make the same things week after week because you don't have time to think.

So this is where my meal planner can be a great help. If you're calorie counting it makes dieting easy. If you're not, you can follow the plan anyway and add a few extras if you like.

It's fine to swap some of the meals for your own favourite dishes, but make sure you base your menu around lean protein and plenty of vegetables and choose smart carbs and good fats, as described in the introduction to this book. This is not a crash plan. It is designed to help you have a healthy diet, while cutting right back on added sugar and empty calories. It also helps to balance your blood sugar so you avoid those weak wobbly moments.

If you do change dishes, check the calories they contain but a few calories more or less each day isn't going to ruin your diet. Most of the recipes in *5 Weeks to Sugar-Free* and *Smart Carbs* will also work well here. And you can have as many green and non-starchy vegetables as you like, so add those in as you like and they'll help to fill you up. Most of these meals are fine for the non-dieters in the family, but you'll probably want to add extra sides for them – such as wholewheat toast with the soups, and brown rice or sweet potato with some of the main dishes. Non-dieters can have more of the yummy cakes and puddings too!

Most of the soups freeze well so make double batches when you can and stash some away for another day. And lots of the salads are ideal for taking to work with you so you can avoid being tempted into the sandwich bar.

While you're following the plan it's important to drink plenty of water. First, water helps to fill you up and reduces the urge to snack or overeat.. You can have tea and coffee – no sugar – but avoid sweet sodas, even the calorie-free ones, because the aim is to retrain your taste buds to enjoy the natural flavours of food and wean yourself off things that are overly sweet. It is best to stay off alcohol for these five weeks too.

Here's what to do

Week 1   Aim for 1,400 kcals a day. That's about 300 kcals for breakfast, 350 for lunch and 550 for your evening meal, plus a snack (about 100 calories) mid-morning and the same in the afternoon.

Week 2   Aim for 1,300 kcals a day That's about 300 kcals for breakfast, 300 for lunch and 500 for your evening meal, plus a snack (about 100 calories) mid-morning and the same in the afternoon.

Weeks 3, 4, 5   Aim for 1,200 kcals a day. That's about 250 kcals for breakfast, 300 for lunch and 450 for your evening meal, plus snacks.

In the weekend menus, we've generally allowed for a slightly bigger breakfast and/or puddings in the evening so dropped the snacks.

Week 1

	Breakfast	Snack	Lunch	Snack	Evening meal
Monday	Porridge + handful of blueberries	Apple	Roasted tomato and red pepper soup and goat cheese toasts	Prune and almond chocolate truffle	Glazed salmon with rainbow vegetables
Tuesday	Berrytastic smoothie	Banana	Broccoli, spelt and orange salad	Carrot and seed cracker with nut butter	Baked roasted tomato risotto + green salad
Wednesday	2 boiled eggs + 1 slice wholemeal toast	Pear	Bean and chorizo soup + 1 slice of seedy soda bread	Chocolate, cherry and almond fudge	Smoked mackerel salad with apple dressing
Thursday	Banana, blueberry and oat smoothie	20g almonds	Chicken, carrot and chickpea salad	20g savoury popcorn	Squash 'spaghetti' with pancetta sauce + green salad
Friday	3 heaped tbsp muesli + 150 milk + handful of raspberries	2 satsumas	Cold tomato soup à la AJ	Prune and almond chocolate truffle	Thai sea bass with coconut rice
Saturday	Plain yoghurt and 200g fresh mango	-	Halloumi and asparagus salad	-	Pork meatballs with pasta and tomato sauce Blackcurrant and mint sorbet
Sunday	½ grapefruit + scrambled eggs (2 medium eggs and 1 tsp butter) + 1 slice of wholemeal toast	-	Spicy chicken salad	-	Lamb casserole with Cheddar and thyme dumplings + green vegetables Chargrilled peaches with orange cream

Week 2

	Breakfast	Snack	Lunch	Snack	Evening meal
Monday	Green pineapple smoothie	Apple	Chicken Caesar salad	Fruit and nut cookie	Grilled tuna with peppers and lentils
Tuesday	3 heaped tbsp muesli + 150 milk + handful of raspberries	20g almonds	Home-made pot noodles	Fresh mango (150g)	Spaghetti with creamy veggie sauce + green salad
Wednesday	Berrytastic smoothie	1 banana	Beetroot and apple soup + 1 wholemeal roll	Prune and almond chocolate truffle	Pan-fried lemon sole with hot tomato salsa
Thursday	2 boiled eggs + 1 slice wholemeal toast	Pear	Nutty greens	Fruit and nut cookie	Stuffed courgette + tomato salad
Friday	Banana, blueberry and oat smoothie	Fruity flapjack	Minty pea soup + 1 wholemeal roll	Spicy squash hummus and raw veg sticks	Pork fillet with mushroom sauce + green beans
Saturday	Porridge + handful of blueberries	-	Sunshine soup + raw veg sticks	-	Chicken, leek and mushroom pie + tenderstem broccoli Frozen chocolate banana popsicles
Sunday	½ grapefruit + scrambled eggs (2 medium eggs and 1 tsp butter) + 1 slice of wholemeal toast	-	Bean and chorizo soup + 1 slice of seedy soda bread	-	Lamb and apricot pilaf + green salad Watermelon, pomegranate and mint granita

Week 3

	Breakfast	Snack	Lunch	Snack	Evening meal
Monday	1 pot of plain yoghurt + 200g fresh pineapple	Carrot and seed cracker and 1 tbsp spicy squash hummus	Cheesy pea fritters and roasted cherry tomatoes	Savoury popcorn	Baked roasted tomato risotto + green salad
Tuesday	2 boiled eggs + 1 slice of wholemeal toast	Apple	Supergreen soup + 1 slice of seedy soda bread	50g olives	Crunchy buttermilk chicken with roasted ratatouille
Wednesday	Green pineapple smoothie	Banana	Halloumi and asparagus salad	Prune and almond chocolate truffle	Cod and pesto parcels + steamed green vegetables
Thursday	3 heaped tbsp muesli + 150 milk + handful of raspberries	20g almonds	Courgette and shrimp salad	1 slice of malt loaf	Squash 'spaghetti' with pancetta sauce
Friday	Berrytastic smoothie	Pear	Red pepper toasties	Sesame kale crisps	Cauliflower 'steaks' with onion and chorizo
Saturday	1 pot of plain yoghurt + 1 banana	-	Minty pea soup + 1 wholemeal roll	-	Slow-cooked pork + Carrot, apple and beetroot slaw Chocolate, honey and raspberry parfait
Sunday	½ grapefruit + scrambled eggs (2 medium eggs and 1 tsp butter) + 1 slice of wholemeal toast	-	Spicy prawn salad	-	Slow-roast short rib ragu + green salad Blackcurrant and mint sorbet

Week 4

	Breakfast	Snack	Lunch	Snack	Evening meal
Monday	3 heaped tbsp muesli + 150ml milk + handful of blueberries	1 oatcake with nut butter	Supergreen soup + 1 small wholemeal roll	2 satsumas	Pan-fried lemon sole with hot tomato salsa
Tuesday	Berrytastic smoothie	Banana	Grilled corn, avocado and feta salad	Fruit and nut cookie	Pork fillet with mushroom sauce + green beans
Wednesday	Green pineapple smoothie	Apple	Baked eggs Florentine	Fresh mango (150g)	Cauliflower 'steaks' with onion and chorizo
Thursday	2 boiled eggs + 1 slice wholemeal toast	1 pear	Broccoli, spelt and orange salad	2 plums	Chicken cacciatore + steamed green vegetables
Friday	1 pot of plain yoghurt + 200g fresh pineapple	2 large plums	Carrot, apple and beetroot slaw + 1 wholewheat pitta	Savoury popcorn	Seared steak with five-bean salad
Saturday	1 slice of wholemeal toast + 2 tsp nut butter + 1 banana	-	Broccoli and hot-smoked salmon tart	-	Crispy lemon thyme chicken with roasted veggies + green salad
Sunday	Scrambled eggs (2 medium eggs and 1 tsp butter) + 40g smoked salmon	-	Red pepper toasties	-	Lamb kebabs with Greek salad + wholemeal pitta

Week 5

	Breakfast	Snack	Lunch	Snack	Evening meal
Monday	1 slice of wholemeal toast + 2 tsp nut butter + 1 banana	Apple	Roasted tomato and red pepper soup with goat cheese toasts	Carrot and seed cracker + 1 tbsp white bean and rosemary dip	Spaghetti with creamy veggie sauce + green salad
Tuesday	3 tbsp sugar-free muesli + 150ml milk + handful of raspberries	20g almonds	Asparagus and dippy eggs	Banana	Seared steak with five-bean salad
Wednesday	Green pineapple smoothie	2 satsumas	Chicken Caesar salad	Sesame kale crisps	Glazed salmon with rainbow vegetables
Thursday	1 pot of plain yoghurt + 200g mango	Fresh mango (150g)	Spicy prawn salad	20g savoury popcorn	Stuffed courgettes
Friday	Berrytastic smoothie	1 pear	Minty pea soup + Carrot and seed cracker	Handful of blueberries	Fish crumble + green salad
Saturday	1 pot of plain yoghurt + 200g mango	-	Roasted beetroot and celeriac salad + carrot and seed cracker	-	Provençal beef casserole + steamed green vegetables
Sunday	2 boiled eggs + 1 slice of wholemeal toast	-	Cucumber noodle, chicken and cashew salad	-	Pork meatballs with pasta and tomato sauce

Index

almonds
Chocolate, cherry and almond fudge 157, 209
Fruit and nut cookies 158, 209
Nut butter 146, 209
Prune and almond chocolate truffles 154, 209
Squidgy banana and pecan tray bake 196, 210

anchovies
Anchovy dressing 88
Warm anchovy dip 150, 209

apples
Apple and cheese scones 153, 209
Apple dressing 80
Apple purée 200
Beetroot and apple soup 40, 205
Carrot, apple and beetroot slaw 121, 208
Carrot, apple and walnut cupcakes 184, 210

apricots, dried
Fruity flapjacks 192, 210
Lamb and apricot pilaf 91, 207
Stuffed courgettes 68, 206

asparagus
Asparagus and dippy eggs 23, 205
Halloumi and asparagus salad 47, 205

aubergine
Roasted ratatouille 87

avocados
Avocados on carrot and seed crackers 138
Grilled corn, avocado and feta salad 48, 205

bananas
Banana, blueberry and oat smoothie 160, 209
Banana, oat and sultana muffins 183, 210
Frozen chocolate banana popsicles 179, 210
Squidgy banana and pecan tray bake 196, 210

beans
Bean and chorizo soup 31, 205
Seared steak with five-bean salad 96, 207
see also cannellini beans; edamame beans

beef
Provençal beef casserole 129, 208
Seared steak with five-bean salad 96, 207
Slow-roast short rib ragu 126, 208

beetroot
Beetroot and apple soup 40, 205
Berrytastic smoothie 160
Carrot, apple and beetroot slaw 121, 208
Chocolate, beetroot and hazelnut tray bake 187, 210
Roasted beetroot and celeriac salad 59, 206

berries, mixed
Berrytastic smoothie 160, 209
Drop scones with fresh berries 176, 210
Berrytastic smoothie 160, 209

biscuits
Fruit and nut cookies 158, 209
Blackcurrant and mint sorbet 180, 210

blueberries
Banana, blueberry and oat smoothie 160, 209

bread
Malt loaf 199, 210
Seedy soda bread 145, 209
see also Crispbreads; Flatbreads; toasts

broccoli
Broccoli and hot-smoked salmon tart 105, 207
Broccoli, spelt and orange salad 51, 206
Fish crumble topping 106
Supergreen soup 39, 205

brownies
Sweet potato and pecan brownies 203, 210

buttermilk
Crunchy buttermilk chicken with roasted ratatouille 87, 207

butternut squash
Butternut and couscous salad 60, 206
Smoked mackerel salad with apple dressing 80, 206
Spicy squash hummus 137, 208
Squash 'spaghetti' with pancetta sauce 95, 207
Sunshine soup 36, 205

cabbage
Nutty greens 28, 205

cake
Courgette, lemon and poppy seed cake 191, 210
Lemon drizzle cake 195, 210
see also cupcakes and tray bakes

cannellini beans
White bean and rosemary dip with tortilla crisps 141, 208

carrots
Carrot and seed crackers 138, 208
Carrot, apple and beetroot slaw 121, 208
Carrot, apple and walnut cupcakes 184, 210
Chicken, carrot and chickpea salad 56, 206
Rainbow vegetables 79
Sunshine soup 36, 205

cashew nuts
Cucumber noodle, chicken and cashew salad 55, 206
Nut butter 146, 209
Nutty greens 28, 205

casseroles
Lamb casserole with Cheddar and thyme dumplings 117, 208
Provençal beef casserole 129, 208

cauliflower
Cauliflower 'steaks' with onion and chorizo 71, 206
Crispy cauli cheese bites 134, 208

cavolo nero
Cauliflower 'steaks' with onion and chorizo 71, 206
Nutty greens 28, 205

celeriac
Carrot, apple and beetroot slaw 121, 208
Roasted beetroot and celeriac salad 59, 206
Chargrilled peaches with orange cream 172, 209

cheese

Apple and cheese scones 153, 209
Baked roasted tomato risotto 67, 206
Cheddar and thyme dumplings 117
Cheesy dip 101
Cheesy pea fritters with roasted cherry tomatoes 20, 205
Cheesy sauce 101
Crispy cauli cheese bites 134, 208
Goat cheese toasts 32
Grilled corn, avocado and feta salad 48, 205
Halloumi and asparagus salad 47, 205
Healthy nachos with tomato salsa 133, 208
Stuffed courgettes 68, 206
see also ricotta
Cheesecake, Strawberry 168, 209
Cheesy dip 134
Cheesy pea fritters with roasted cherry tomatoes 20, 205
Cheesy sauce 101
chicken
Chicken cacciatore 114, 208
Chicken Caesar salad 88, 207
Chicken, carrot and chickpea salad 56, 206
Chicken, leek and mushroom pie 113, 207
Crispy lemon thyme chicken with roasted veggies 110, 207
Crunchy buttermilk chicken with roasted ratatouille 87, 207
Cucumber noodle, chicken and cashew salad 55, 206
Home-made pot noodles 27, 205
Spicy chicken salad 63, 206
see also Nutty greens
chickpeas
Chicken, carrot and chickpea salad 56, 206
Spicy squash hummus 137, 208
chocolate
Chocolate, beetroot and hazelnut tray bake 187, 210
Chocolate, cherry and almond fudge 157, 209
Chocolate, honey and raspberry parfait 175, 209
Frozen chocolate banana popsicles 179, 210

Prune and almond chocolate truffles 154, 209
Sweet potato and pecan brownies 203, 210
chorizo
Bean and chorizo soup 31, 205
Cauliflower 'steaks' with onion and chorizo 71, 206
coconut milk
Coconut rice 109
Raspberry, coconut and lime panna cotta 167, 209
Supergreen soup 39, 205
Coconut rice 109
cod
Cod and pesto parcels 75, 206
Fish crumble 106, 207
Coffee and walnut tray bake 188, 210
cookies
Fruit and nut cookies 158, 209
corn cobs
Grilled corn, avocado and feta salad 48, 205
Coulis, Raspberry 167
courgettes
Courgette and shrimp salad 52, 206
Courgette, lemon and poppy seed cake 191, 210
Rainbow vegetables 79
Roasted ratatouille 87
Stuffed courgettes 68, 206
see also Squash 'spaghetti'
couscous
Butternut and couscous salad 60, 206
crackers
Carrot and seed crackers 138, 208
Crispbreads, Giant 149, 209
Crispy cauli cheese bites 134, 208
Crispy lemon thyme chicken with roasted veggies 110, 207
Croutons 43
Crunchy buttermilk chicken with roasted ratatouille 87, 207
cucumber
Cucumber noodle, chicken and cashew salad 55, 206
Greek salad 118
Tzatziki 118
cupcakes

Carrot, apple and walnut cupcakes 184, 210
dates
Chocolate, cherry and almond fudge 157, 209
Fruity flapjacks 192, 210
Prune and almond chocolate truffles 154, 209
dips
Cheesy dip 134
Warm anchovy dip 150, 209
White bean and rosemary dip with tortilla crisps 141, 208
Drop scones with fresh berries 176, 210
duck, smoked
Duck, carrot and chickpea salad 56, 206
edamame beans
Halloumi and asparagus salad 47, 205
eggs
Asparagus and dippy eggs 23, 205
Baked eggs Florentine 24, 205
filo pastry
Chicken, leek and mushroom pie 113, 207
Spinach and ricotta filo parcels 102, 207
fish
Broccoli and hot-smoked salmon tart 105, 207
Cod and pesto parcels 75, 206
Fish crumble 106, 207
Glazed salmon with rainbow vegetables 79, 206
Grilled tuna with peppers and lentils 84, 207
Pan-fried lemon sole with hot tomato salsa 76, 206
Salmon and sweet potato fishcakes 83, 207
Smoked mackerel salad with apple dressing 80, 206
Thai sea bass with coconut rice 109, 207
Flapjacks, Fruity 192, 210
Flatbreads 121, 208

fritters
  Cheesy pea fritters with roasted
    cherry tomatoes 20, 205
Frozen chocolate banana popsicles
    179, 210
Fruit and nut cookies 158, 209
Fruity flapjacks 192, 210
fudge
  Chocolate, cherry and almond fudge
    157, 209

Giant crispbreads 149, 209
Gingerbread, Sticky 200, 210
Glazed salmon with rainbow
    vegetables 79, 206
Goat cheese toasts 32
granita
  Watermelon, pomegranate and mint
    granita 171, 209
Greek salad 118
Green pineapple smoothie 161,
    209

haddock, smoked
  Fish crumble 106, 207
Halloumi and asparagus salad 47, 205
hazelnuts
  Chocolate, beetroot and hazelnut
    tray bake 187, 210
  Fruit and nut cookies 158, 209
  Nut butter 146, 209
  see also Prune and almond
    chocolate truffles
Healthy nachos with tomato salsa 133,
    208
Herb dressing 55
hummus
  Spicy squash hummus 137, 208

icing 184
  Chocolate icing 187
  Coffee icing 188
  Lemon icing 191

kale
  Nutty greens 28, 205
  Sesame kale crisps 142, 208
  Supergreen soup 39, 205
kebabs
  Lamb kebabs with Greek salad 118,
    208

lamb
  Lamb and apricot pilaf 91, 207
  Lamb casserole with Cheddar and
    thyme dumplings 117, 208
  Lamb kebabs with Greek salad 118,
    208
lasagne
  Tortilla lasagne 101, 207
leeks
  Chicken, leek and mushroom pie
    113, 207
  Spaghetti with creamy veggie sauce
    72, 206
lemons
  Lemon drizzle cake 195, 210
  Lemon icing 191
lemon sole
  Pan-fried lemon sole with hot
    tomato salsa 76, 206
lentils, cooking 84

mackerel, smoked
  Smoked mackerel salad with apple
    dressing 80, 206
Malt loaf 199, 210
meatballs
  Pork meatballs with pasta and
    tomato sauce 125, 208
mint
  Blackcurrant and mint sorbet 180,
    210
  Mint oil 35
  Minty pea soup 35, 205
muffins
  Banana, oat and sultana muffins 183,
    210
mushrooms
  Chicken, leek and mushroom pie
    113, 207
  Pork fillet with mushroom sauce 92,
    207

nachos
  Healthy nachos with tomato salsa
    133, 208
noodles
  Home-made pot noodles 27, 205
nuts
  Fruit and nut cookies 158, 209
  Nut butters 146, 209
  see also cashew nuts; hazelnuts;
    pecan nuts; walnuts

Nutty greens 28, 205

oats
  Banana, blueberry and oat smoothie
    160, 209
  Banana, oat and sultana muffins 183,
    210
  Fruity flapjacks 192, 210
oranges
  Broccoli, spelt and orange salad 51,
    206
  Chargrilled peaches with orange
    cream 172, 209

Pan-fried lemon sole with hot tomato
    salsa 76, 206
pancetta
  Squash 'spaghetti' with pancetta
    sauce 95, 207
panna cotta
  Raspberry, coconut and lime panna
    cotta 167, 209
parfait
  Chocolate, honey and raspberry
    parfait 175, 209
pasta
  Pork meatballs with pasta and
    tomato sauce 125, 208
  Slow-roast short rib ragu 126, 208
  Spaghetti with creamy veggie sauce
    72, 206
peaches
  Chargrilled peaches with orange
    cream 172, 209
peas
  Cheesy pea fritters with roasted
    cherry tomatoes 20, 205
  Minty pea soup 35, 205
pecan nuts
  Fruit and nut cookies 158, 209
  Squidgy banana and pecan tray bake
    196, 210
  Sweet potato and pecan brownies
    203, 210
peppers
  Bean and chorizo soup 31, 205
  Chicken cacciatore 114, 208
  Cold tomato soup à la AJ 43, 205
  Grilled tuna with peppers and lentils
    84, 207
  Rainbow vegetables 79
  Red pepper toasties 19, 205

Roasted tomato and red pepper soup
with goat cheese toasts 32, 205

pesto
Cod and pesto parcels 75, 206

pilaf
Lamb and apricot pilaf 91, 207

pineapple
Green pineapple smoothie 161,
209

pomegranate juice/seeds
Watermelon, pomegranate and mint
granita 171, 209

popsicles
Frozen chocolate banana popsicles
179, 210

pork
Pork fillet with mushroom sauce 92,
207
Pork meatballs with pasta and
tomato sauce 125, 208
Slow-cooked pulled pork 120, 208
Pot noodles, Home-made 27, 205

prawns and shrimps
Courgette and shrimp salad 52, 206
Home-made pot noodles 27, 205
Prawn, carrot and chickpea salad 56,
206
Spicy prawn salad 63, 206
Provençal beef casserole 129, 208

prunes
Fruit and nut cookies 158, 209
Malt loaf 199, 210
Prune and almond chocolate truffles
154, 209
Sweet potato and pecan brownies
203, 210

pumpkin seeds
Seed sprinkle topping (for soup) 36

quinoa
Fish crumble 106, 207
Roasted beetroot and celeriac salad
59, 206

raspberries
Chocolate, honey and raspberry
parfait 175, 209
Raspberry, coconut and lime panna
cotta 167, 209
Raspberry coulis 167
Ratatouille, Roasted 87
Red pepper toasties 19, 205

rice
Baked roasted tomato risotto 67, 206
Coconut rice 109
Lamb and apricot pilaf 91, 207

ricotta
Red pepper toasties 19, 205
Spinach and ricotta filo parcels 102,
207

salads
Broccoli, spelt and orange salad 51,
206
Butternut and couscous salad 60,
206
Chicken Caesar salad 88, 207
Chicken, carrot and chickpea salad
56, 206
Courgette and shrimp salad 52, 206
Cucumber noodle, chicken and
cashew salad 55, 206
Greek salad 118
Grilled corn, avocado and feta salad
48, 205
Halloumi and asparagus salad 47,
205
Roasted beetroot and celeriac salad
59, 206
Seared steak with five-bean salad 96,
207
Smoked mackerel salad with apple
dressing 80, 206
Spicy prawn or chicken salad 63, 206

salmon
Broccoli and hot-smoked salmon tart
105, 207
Fish crumble 106, 207
Glazed salmon with rainbow
vegetables 79, 206
Salmon and sweet potato fishcakes
83, 207

salsa
Hot tomato salsa 76
Tomato salsa 133

sauces
Cheesy sauce 101
Creamy veggie sauce 72
Mushroom sauce 92
Pancetta sauce 95
Tomato sauce 125
Vegetable sauce 101

scones
Apple and cheese scones 153, 209

Drop scones with fresh berries 176,
210

sea bass
Thai sea bass with coconut rice 109,
207
Seared steak with five-bean salad 96,
207

seeds, mixed
Carrot and seed crackers 138, 208
Courgette, lemon and poppy seed
cake 191, 210
Fruit and nut cookies 158, 209
Green pineapple smoothie 161, 209
Seedy soda bread 145, 209
see also pumpkin seeds; Sesame
kale crisps
Seedy soda bread 145, 209
Sesame kale crisps 142, 208
shrimps see prawns and shrimps

slaw
Carrot, apple and beetroot slaw 121,
208
Slow-cooked pulled pork 120, 208
Slow-roast short rib ragu 126, 208
Smoked mackerel salad with apple
dressing 80, 206

smoothies
Banana, blueberry and oat smoothie
160, 209
Berrytastic smoothie 160, 209
Green pineapple smoothie 161, 209
Watermelon, strawberry and mint
smoothie 161, 209
Soda bread, Seedy 145, 209
sole see lemon sole

sorbet
Blackcurrant and mint sorbet 180,
210

soups
Bean and chorizo soup 31, 205
Beetroot and apple soup 40, 205
Cold tomato soup à la AJ 43, 205
Minty pea soup 35, 205
Roasted tomato and red pepper soup
with goat cheese toasts 32, 205
Sunshine soup 36, 205
Supergreen soup 39, 205
Spaghetti with creamy veggie sauce 72,
206

spelt
Broccoli, spelt and orange salad 51,
206

spelt flour
  Banana, oat and sultana muffins 183, 210
  Apple and cheese scones 153, 209
  Cheddar and thyme dumplings 117
  Courgette, lemon and poppy seed cake 191, 210
  Drop scones with fresh berries 176, 210
  Flatbreads 121, 208
  Giant crispbreads 149, 209
  Malt loaf 199, 210
  see also cakes; tray bakes
Spicy chicken salad 63, 206
Spicy squash hummus 137, 208
spinach
  Baked eggs Florentine 24, 205
  Cauliflower 'steaks' with onion and chorizo 71, 206
  Green pineapple smoothie 161, 209
  Spinach and ricotta filo parcels 102, 207
  Supergreen soup 39, 205
squash *see* butternut squash
Squash 'spaghetti' with pancetta sauce 95, 207
Squidgy banana and pecan tray bake 196, 210
stews *see* casseroles
Sticky gingerbread 200, 210
stir-fry
  Nutty greens 28, 205
strawberries
  Strawberry cheesecake 168, 209
  Watermelon, strawberry and mint smoothie 161, 209
Stuffed courgettes 68, 206

Sunshine soup 36, 205
Supergreen soup 39, 205
sweet potatoes
  Salmon and sweet potato fishcakes 83, 207
  Sweet potato and pecan brownies 203, 210

tart
  Broccoli and hot-smoked salmon tart 105, 207
Thai sea bass with coconut rice 109, 207
toasts
  Goat cheese toasts 32
  Red pepper toasties 19, 205
tomatoes
  Baked roasted tomato risotto 67, 206
  Bean and chorizo soup 31, 205
  Cold tomato soup à la AJ 43, 205
  Greek salad 118
  Hot tomato salsa 76
  Roasted tomato and red pepper soup with goat cheese toasts 32, 205
  Tomato dressing 47
  Tomato salsa 133
  Tomato sauce 125
tortillas
  Healthy nachos with tomato salsa 133, 208
  Tortilla lasagne 101, 207
  White bean and rosemary dip with tortilla crisps 141, 208
tray bakes
  Chocolate, beetroot and hazelnut tray bake 187, 210
  Coffee and walnut tray bake 188, 210

  Squidgy banana and pecan tray bake 196, 210
truffles
  Prune and almond chocolate truffles 154, 209
tuna
  Grilled tuna with peppers and lentils 84, 207
Tzatziki 118

vanilla extract/vanilla powder 168
vegetables, mixed
  Chicken cacciatore 114, 208
  Crispy lemon thyme chicken with roasted veggies 110, 207
  Home-made pot noodles 27, 205
  Rainbow vegetables 79
  Vegetable sauces 72, 101

walnuts
  Carrot, apple and walnut cupcakes 184, 210
  Coffee and walnut tray bake 188, 210
watermelon
  Watermelon, pomegranate and mint granita 171, 209
  Watermelon, strawberry and mint smoothie 161, 209
White bean and rosemary dip with tortilla crisps 141, 208

yoghurt
  Banana, blueberry and oat smoothie 160, 209
  Berrytastic smoothie 160, 209
  Dressing for slaw 121
  Tzatziki 118

Thanks team – love you lots

Yet again you've helped me put together a great book and I've loved every minute of it.

A whole bundle of hugs to Anna Burges-Lumsden, who not only developed the recipes for me but also cooked all the food for the shoots and made it look totally amazing. Andrew Hayes-Watkins is the best fun to work with and has done the food proud. Helen Ewing, Clare Sivell, Abi Hartshorne and Sarah Birks have all worked their socks off to make the book look utterly beautiful, and as always Fiona Hunter has provided nutritional advice and manages to explain difficult things like blood sugar in a way I can understand. Elise See Tai and Vicki Robinson have given stalwart help with proofreading and indexing. And the wonderful Fiona McIntosh and Katie Horrocks in the Orion production department have ensured the whole thing came together to make a book to be proud of.

Angie Smith, Cheryl Phelps-Gardiner and Michael Douglas – totally love you all for helping me scrub up well. I love you guys so much.

Amanda Harris and Jinny Johnson – thank you both for keeping it all together and on track while still smiling. Seriously – you are the best.

To everyone at James Grant, especially Rowan, Emily and Hayley – thank you all for your great support and general wonderfulness. I would be rubbish without you.

Matthew – you are my very funny, kind, supportive rock. Love you so much. And to my bestest, most honest critics – Holly (you're rapidly turning into a better cook than me), Tilly and Chester! Thank you for your lovely help in the kitchen. Love you all to the moon and back.

xxxxxx